# How to Make a Quick Fortune:
# New Ways to Build Wealth Fast

## Other Books by Tyler G. Hicks

*How to Build a Second-Income Fortune in Your Spare Time*

*Smart Money Shortcuts to Becoming Rich*

*How to Start Your Own Business on a Shoestring and
Make up to $100,000 a Year*

*How to Borrow Your Way to a Great Fortune*

*Magic Mind Secrets for Building Great Riches Fast*

# How to Make a Quick Fortune: New Ways to Build Wealth Fast

*Tyler G. Hicks*

Parker Publishing Company, Inc., West Nyack, N.Y.

Library of Congress Cataloging in Publication Data

Hicks, Tyler Gregory
    How to make a quick fortune.

    Bibliography:  p.
    1.  Business.  2.  Success.  I.  Title.
HF5386.H4853        658.4'09        73-14795
ISBN 0-13-423384-0

Printed in the United States of America

# How to Build Your Fortune Anywhere

You *can* get rich today anywhere—starting with zero cash! And this book quickly shows you exactly how to get rich anywhere—step-by-step—without leaving your own home. Or, if you wish, you can roam wherever you please, at your own pace, enjoying new vistas and people while the profits roll into your company and your pockets.

Yes, *you can* get rich anywhere. How do I know? Because I've helped thousands of people everywhere get rich in many different businesses. Most of these people began with little, or no, cash. And I haven't been exactly a slouch myself—if you could glance over my bank accounts, I think you'd say that I'm: (a) successful, (b) busy, (c) an international character with friends and business acquaintances everywhere.

## Get rich without a big investment

I'm a strong believer in a number of important practical and profitable business concepts and techniques. Briefly, I firmly and strongly believe in:

- Making *you* rich as quickly as possible
- Building your riches on the smallest cash investment (zero cash if possible)
- Using other people's money to finance your wealth building
- Creating great wealth for you without the need for a factory, big payroll, and so forth.
- Being as helpful as possible to you in a personal way
- Using "paper" facilities to build your wealth

And that, friend—in essence—is what this book is all about—the building of great wealth quickly for *you* with little more than a mailing address and some pieces of paper. You don't even need a telephone. (I've run a highly profitable business for years without a phone—I figure that this approach keeps the customers out of my private life!) Throughout this book I put great stress on the zero-cash, other-people's-money (OPM) approach.

### Know what can make you rich

In the "paper" businesses (such as mail order, export-import, financial broker, consultant, real estate, and the like) which I recommend you consider running to make yourself rich fast, you hardly even need an office. What you do need, and what I'm sure you have is a:

- Burning desire to get rich
- Willingness to work hard
- Creative approach to solving problems
- Sensible head with eyes and ears to see and hear with
- Quick ability to learn from other people

These characteristics can make you richer sooner than you ever thought possible. All you need do is read the book you are now holding and put my hints and methods to work. Now you *know* what kind of an outlook can make you rich within a few months or a few years, depending on how hard you work!

### Use smart-money riches techniques

You could, possibly, get rich digging ditches. But ditch digging is not, in my opinion, a smart way for *you* to get rich. True, you may like the exercise. But I'd rather see you get rich in another, easier, more congenial business and have you take your exercise on the tennis court, golf course, in your private swimming pool, or on your sparkling new yacht.

So I urge you to consider my zero-cash smart-money riches techniques. Using these techniques you will:

- Get richer faster
- Become happier
- Gain control over yourself and others
- Help those in need
- Give your family all they want
- Make the world a better place

If these rewards—and many others—interest you, then read on to learn how I propose to put enormous riches within your easy reach. Thousands of others begin to build riches every year using my methods. So why shouldn't you? I will also show you what kinds of businesses can make you wealthy on zero cash so you'll know—from this day on—how to live the happy and fruitful life you've always wanted, and to which you are entitled. To make things easier for you, specific names and addresses of business data sources are given throughout the book.

## Take your magic steps to great wealth

The easy zero-cash methods for building fast wealth that I would like to have you consider trying can make you rich *anywhere*—from east to west, north to south, continent to continent. In the chapters that make up this book I show you how to:

- Get rich quickly anywhere on zero cash
- Mail your way to enormous wealth
- Go international for your mail riches
- Export your way to a great fortune
- Import worldwide products and prosper
- Be a finder, consultant or broker for big fees
- Borrow your way to great wealth
- Use no-capital ways to build your fortune
- Get all the business help you need
- Work at home for big profits
- Make real estate make you a millionaire
- Become an "instant" millionaire today
- Franchise your way to riches

Each of the methods I show you is PROVEN, PRACTICAL, and PROFITABLE! I skip long-hair, involved theories and give you the down-to-earth step-by-step methods you should consider following to build great riches fast.

### Take the word of a pro

So come with me, my good friend, be you a Beginning Wealth Builder (BWB), or an Advanced Wealth Builder (AWB), and I'll show you how a pro hits the big money quickly. You can easily do the same—if you enjoy working hard every day of the year. Once you've hit the big money, you can relax and take it easy for the rest of your life.

You *can* get rich *now, today, here,* by using the powerful zero-cash, no-capital "paper" methods given you in this book. It will cost you little more than your time and a few stamps to start building enormous private wealth. So why not start, here and now? Your zooming riches will soon show you that you, too, can get richer, sooner than you ever dreamed! Come with me, good friend, and learn how—*now.*

Tyler G. Hicks

# Contents

2.    **Mail Your Way to Enormous Wealth** *(cont.)*

**14.  Build Millions from Pennies in Your Own Business** *(cont.)*

*facts from others . What's a successful franchise idea? . Nine magic steps to getting started in franchising . Now sell hard and truthfully . Help your franchise and yourself to big profits . Expand your business and your income*

*Get more people to build your wealth . Get synergy to multiply your fortune . How beginners build success in franchising*

# 1

# You <u>Can</u> Get Rich Anywhere

You *can* get rich, starting this instant, and in the very spot where you now sit, stand, or lie! How can I say this? Because I personally know—and will tell you about people, much like yourself—who've built enormous fortunes in:

- Their home basement, attic, or garage
- A city apartment
- A maximum-security prison cell
- The cabin of a seagoing tanker
- A house trailer
- A ski lodge in the mountains
- A borrowed business office
- An alley in a small city

Yes, these people, and thousands of others, have a wonderful lesson to teach us all. This lesson, which their lives give us, is:

> You can get rich anywhere, if you really want to get
> rich, and if you are willing to work toward your goal.

In this chapter I'll show you how to prove to yourself that *you* can get rich anywhere in the world.

## Make this place your place

Almost everyone has been to a party or other gathering when some new guests arrived and seemed to "take over" the place with their presence and talk. They made the party "their place." And perhaps you—or other people there—felt a twinge of envy, wishing that you could get the same attention.

You can, you know, get much the same attention—if you want it. But what's more, I'd like to show you how to make any place *your* place for earning a BIG INCOME while getting the attention you might be seeking. Just remember this fact:

> No matter how ugly, crippled, or handicapped a rich person is, he or she is still the center of attraction no matter where he or she goes, if people know about his or her wealth.

*You* can make *this* place *your* place for doing business. And where is *this* place? It can be anywhere you want to work. *You* are the boss in *this* place. So you can pick it as you wish. Places you might pick are:

- Your home
- A local restaurant
- A country club
- Your boat
- A trailer
- A commuter train
- A bus
- An airport waiting room
- An office
- An airplane

The main point I'd like you to keep in mind is this:

> Any place you choose to get rich—anywhere in this great world of ours—is the place where you can quickly build enormous wealth.

Now let's get on with getting *you* started on the road toward *your* great wealth.

### Know your lucky assets

To get rich anywhere—be it in the United States, Europe, Asia, Australia, Africa—you need the following seven lucky assets.

## FORTUNE-BUILDING ASSETS

| YOUR ASSET | YOUR USE OF YOUR ASSET |
|---|---|
| 1. Time | Working hours to make your product or give your service |
| 2. Energy | To power your mind and body to do the work needed to build your fortune |
| 3. Know-how | To give your customers and clients what they can't get from others |
| 4. Success drive | To push you onward and upward |
| 5. Self-confidence | To help yourself overcome problems you're sure to meet |
| 6. Follow-through | To keep yourself working until you hit the big money |
| 7. Nimbleness | To help you adapt to changing conditions and places |

*You* have *all* these seven lucky assets right now! "How do you know I have all these seven assets?" you ask. Because, good friend, I've met thousands of BWB's (Beginning Wealth Builders) and each taught me something about himself or herself. One fact which always stands out about any BWB is:

> Soon-to-be-successful BWB's often read books and articles on how to make money quickly and easily. The BWB reads these books and articles to keep himself charged up and motivated to do more.

Since you are reading *this* book—which tells you how to get richer, quicker, anywhere—it follows that you are soon to be successful! And most soon-to-be-successful BWB's I've met have the assets listed. So it follows that you, too, have these seven lucky assets!

### Put your assets to work

Now let's look at *your* assets and see how *you* can put them to work starting here and now. You'll soon see that you're much better off and nearer your fortune than you thought you were! And even if you're short of any of these important assets, you can take action today to start rebuilding them.

Now get a sheet of paper and write down *your* answers to the questions in the following checklist. DO NOT WRITE IN YOUR BOOK—you may want to change your answers at a later date and it will be difficult to do this without marring the page.

### MY RICHES ASSETS CHECKLIST

1. Time

Effective today, _(date)_, I will devote _(enter number)_ hours per day to building my fortune.

2. Energy

Today I think I _(am; am not)_ devoting enough energy to build my fortune quickly. If I am not, I will by _(date)_ start devoting more energy to building great wealth for myself. And, if I think it is necessary, I will get a complete physical checkup by _(date)_ to learn how I can increase my energy reserves.

3. Know-how

Starting today _(date)_, I will spend _(number)_ minutes a day reading about my future business to improve my know-how of it.

4. Success drive

Right now my success drive is _(strong; weak)_ If it's weak, I'll take the steps given later in this chapter by _(date)_ to strengthen my success drive.

5. Self-confidence

In my opinion, I have _(strong; weak)_ self-confidence. If my self-confidence is weak, I'll take the steps given later in this chapter by _(date)_ to increase it.

6. Follow-through

I have _(strong; weak)_ follow-through. Since follow-through is one of the key traits needed for success, I'll do everything possible to strengthen *my* follow-through, starting on _(date)_.

7. Nimbleness

"Jack be nimble; Jack be quick," is part of a famous nursery rhyme. This rhyme is true also for your business. So if you are a slow-starter and slow-mover, consider putting a little more zest into your actions. You'll find that the faster you move in business, the surer you become and the greater will be your success!

## Beef up your wealth success drive now

Of the seven lucky assets you've just read about, three are part of your personality. And these three, namely your:

- Success drive
- Self-confidence, and
- Follow-through

are key factors in your *wealth success* or your *money drive.* Strengthening all of these personality assets can put you into the big money faster than you think. Here are your simple techniques for beefing up these traits *and* your wealth success or money drive.

## PUT YOUR WEALTH SUCCESS DRIVE INTO HIGH GEAR

Never knock wealth success. Tell yourself every day that wealth success is:

- Positive
- Beneficial
- Useful
- Fun
- Admired

- Creative
- Healthful
- Worthwhile
- Lasting
- Profitable

The more often you tell yourself about the benefits of wealth success, the stronger your success drive will become. And a strong success drive will help you build your fortune anywhere, any time. Remember: *If you can imagine yourself doing something, then you can actually do it!*

## IMPROVE YOUR SELF-CONFIDENCE

You're the most important person in the world to yourself! So you *must* learn to:

- Like yourself
- Accept yourself
- Believe in yourself
- Have confidence in your skills
- Take command of yourself
- Plan and control your future

Now here's a practical program to improve your self-confidence and put an improved *you* to work for *yourself* in your business life. You'll find that in this improvement program you go through a joyous, fun-filled nine-step process.

## NINE STEPS TO GREATER SELF-CONFIDENCE

1. Recognize that increased self-confidence helps you every moment, everywhere. Remind yourself of this *every* day.
2. List your good traits and skills.
3. Note how rarely *your* traits and skills are found in one person.
4. Welcome your goodness.
5. Decide to improve your skills.
6. Get interested in your work.
7. Improve your finances by working harder and saving more.
8. See yourself as you really are.
9. Like yourself because you're the only *you* you have!

Once your self-confidence improves, you'll find that your life is easier. You'll:

- Work faster
- Accomplish more
- Make fewer mistakes
- Earn more money
- Be happier
- Create more good things

Improving your self-confidence makes you a:

- Self-starter
- Self-regenerator
- Self-reliant person

## BUILD STRONG FOLLOW-THROUGH

In my many business activities I meet thousands of BWB's. Many are enthusiastic and willing to work. But one problem many of these BWB's have is *follow-through*. They can't stick with, or to, an idea long enough to prove it out. So almost everything they do fails.

Don't you be a BWB with weak follow-through. Resolve today that you will:

- Pick your business deal carefully
- Make mental "dry runs" before starting any deal
- Carefully check out every deal in advance
- Stick with an idea for as long as possible
- Never give up a good idea—keep trying for years and years

### USE AUTO-SUGGESTION TO BUILD WEALTH SUCCESS

The easiest way to put the just-listed hints into action so that you begin to profit from them *now*—this very day—is to get a 3x5-inch card and write on it these key words:

- Tell
- Like
- Accept
- Believe

- Have
- Take
- Plan
- Follow

*Each day* repeat the key thought which each word suggests to you, as I gave them to you, or:

- Tell      yourself about the benefits of wealth success.
- Like      yourself—you're the most *important,* and the *only* you you'll ever have!
- Accept  yourself—say hello to the greatest person in this world!
- Believe  in yourself—you can really do one hundred times more than you think you can!
- Have     confidence in the skills you have today and the new ones you'll learn tomorrow!
- Take     command of yourself—become the master of your future, the captain of your life!
- Plan     and control your future; make the world yours!
- Follow   through; don't give up; finish what you start!

By repeating these thoughts to yourself—I recommend that you repeat them aloud to yourself in the privacy of a closed room— you build a positive go-power deep in your subconscious. In just a few days, auto-suggestion takes over. You then begin to *act* as though you really believe what you told yourself. And since all of the suggestions are positive, you soon begin to *do* more in life, *accomplish* more, and then, *earn* more. All by just thinking the *right* thoughts *every* day of the year!

## Remember—anywhere means anywhere!

Yes, good friend, you *can* get rich anywhere, if you listen to your pal, Ty Hicks. Here are some actual cases of places where real, live people, just like you and me, have grown rich. You can do the same—today, here, now!

### ACTUAL PLACES AND THE REAL FORTUNES BUILT THERE

| | |
|---|---|
| Home garage | One of the world's largest toy firms started in a backyard garage. So did the nation's largest management training group. |
| Private home | What is today the world's largest computer consulting firm was started in the bedroom of a suburban home. And a large mail-order business was started on the kitchen table of a city apartment. |
| School classroom | Europe's largest privately-owned correspondence school, which today has 90,000 students, was started in the corner of a classroom by a bored teacher who wanted something interesting to do between classes. And a large management consulting firm started in the basement laboratory of a small engineering college. |
| Prison cell | Numerous profitable best-selling books have been written in prison cells—some by men living under the shadow of the death penalty. Other prisoners have operated profitable clipping services, mail-order businesses, and similar activities in their cells. |
| Other places | There is no limit to the places where you can get rich—be it a small town, a large city, the desert, or the high seas. People regularly—and routinely—get rich every year, everywhere. There's no reason why you shouldn't also get rich anywhere *you* choose. |

## Size up your location

Although it's true that you *can* get rich anywhere, you may have to make allowances for *your* location. Thus, if you're living in a small town and you want to sell products throughout the world, you may have to use:

- Mail order
- Sales reps
- Export agents
- Space advertising
- Overseas salesmen

to make the sales you seek. But no matter what methods you pick, just remember:

> It is easy for anyone who sets his mind to it to build
> great riches quickly, starting with a good idea.

To make really big money, you must be able to pick the best way to take your ideas to market from your particular location. Later chapters show you *exactly* how to do this.

"But," you say, "*I* don't have *any* good ideas to take to market. How can *I* get rich?"

Plenty of BWB's ask me this question *every* week of the year and my reply always is: "That's an easy question to answer!"

Why? Because I've helped plenty of No-Ideas Beginners (NIB's I call them) get started using other people's *good* ideas and *good* money. To show you that what I say is true, I'll now give you one way BWB's can get good ideas free of charge. It's called the *Golden Idea Route*. You'll read about plenty of other ways of easily getting great wealth-building ideas in later chapters.

## Go the golden idea route

Let's say that you're the Mr., Mrs., or Miss NIB we just mentioned. If you don't find that flattering, then let's say you have a friend named NIB. Good ideas for "making a big bundle of money quickly" are difficult for a NIB—a No-Idea Beginner to find. So what can such a person do to get good business ideas quickly?

One key step he can take is to get interested in a business in which ideas are important. Such typical businesses are:

- Product and process licensing
- Industrial and consumer advertising
- Mail order sales
- Import-export

Let's take a look at the first business—product and process licensing—to see how it might help a typical NIB.

To start, imagine that we are talking about the problem of getting good business ideas. If we were, I'd say to you: "To get good business ideas, I suggest that the typical NIB think about becoming a licensing agent."

"Please explain what you mean," you reply with a trace of interest in your voice. Just read on, good friend, to learn how you might plant *your* money tree. We'll begin to grow your fortune with an easy definition, namely that:

Licensing is the means used by one firm to allow another firm to make, use, or sell a product, process, service, or other item which the first firm owns or controls. Thus, Company A might license Company B to make a patented toy, use a chemical process, or sell a trademarked device invented by the engineers and scientists at Company A. Licensing may be arranged between firms in either the same or in different countries—for example, the United States and England, France, Germany, or other likely places.

A *licensing agent* is a freelancer who arranges license deals between firms both at home and overseas. As a licensing agent you can work:

- When you want to
- Where you want to
- How you want to

Your pay for the work you do as a licensing agent can either be: (1) a fixed one-time payment which you receive when the license agreement is signed, or (2) a percentage of the royalty paid by firm B to firm A for each unit firm B sells. I advise most beginning licensing agents to start with a few fixed one-time payment deals to build up their capital. Then, as their capital builds up in a safe bank account, they can gradually shift to percentage of the royalty. Meanwhile, of course, they're getting many business ideas from their work.

"But," you ask, "how does becoming a licensing agent make up for not having ideas?" Here's your answer.

As a licensing agent you can deal with hundreds of firms at home and around the world—almost exclusively by mail. The ideas developed by the key people of these firms—engineers, scientists, accountants, and others—become *your* ideas to market. Thus, in one day you might be licensing by mail the ideas, products, patents, copyrights, or tradenames of companies in the United States, England, France, Germany, Sweden, or Denmark.

And a beautiful feature of these deals and of being a licensing agent is that you can pick the items that you want to license. Thus, if toys interest you, they can be your licensing specialty. The same is true, of course, for boats, autos, electronic equipment, and so on. So you can, as a licensing agent:

- Pick your business
- Start your business for less than $50
- Get thousands of ideas from others
- Work with the best people
- Earn big money

And—best of all—you'll do all, or almost all, your selling by mail. Rarely will you have to visit a factory or call on a customer. Handling these mail sales will provide you with a steady flow of rich new ideas for your business.

## Making it big can be easy

Yes, making it big *can* be easy—*if you* know how! And this book tells you—and shows you—how. I've just shown you one way (as a licensing agent). "But," you say, "how can I get more info on becoming a licensing agent?"

That's an easy question to answer. Just read some of the booklets (many of which are *free*) that I recommend to you. But before giving you a list of helpful reference reading on becoming a licensing agent, I'd like to explain what I've done for you in the book you are now reading.

In this book, as in my previous five money books, I plan to give you many leads on useful publications which I think would be helpful to you. Where possible, I will list *FREE* pamphlets, brochures, and books first. Following this, you will often find lists or mentions of helpful publications which are sold for various prices. Where the price is known, it will be listed.

Returning to your interest in becoming a licensing agent, you may find the following publications helpful:

### FROM THE SMALL BUSINESS ADMINISTRATION (SBA)

## Free management aids

Know Your Patenting Procedures, #49
Business from Unpatentable Ideas, #53
Exporting for Profit, #121
Expanding Sales Through Franchising, #182
Marketing Planning Guidelines, #194
Expand Overseas Sales, #199

## Free marketers' aids

Checklist for Going Into Business, #71
Sales Potential and Market Share, #112

## Free bibliographies

Selling by Mail Order, #3
Marketing Research Procedures, #9

You can obtain these free publications by writing to the nearest SBA office in the following list.

### SBA FIELD OFFICE ADDRESSES

Boston                    Massachusetts 02203, John Fitzgerald Kennedy Federal Building

| Holyoke | Massachusetts 01040, 326 Appleton Street |
|---|---|
| Augusta | Maine 04330, Federal Building, U.S. Post Office, 40 Western Avenue |
| Concord | New Hampshire 03301, 55 Pleasant Street |
| Hartford | Connecticut 06103, Federal Office Building, 450 Maine Street |
| Montpelier | Vermont 05601, Federal Building, 2nd Floor, 87 State Street |
| Providence | Rhode Island 02903, 702 Smith Building, 57 Eddy Street |
| New York | New York 10007, 26 Federal Plaza, Room 3930 |
| Hato Rey | Puerto Rico 00919, 255 Ponce De Leon Avenue |
| Newark | New Jersey 07102, 970 Broad Street, Room 1636 |
| Syracuse | New York 13202, Hunter Plaza, Fayette & Salina Streets |
| Buffalo | New York 14203, Federal Building, Room 9, 121 Ellicott Street |
| Albany | New York 12297, 91 State Street |
| Philadelphia | Bala Cynwyd, Pennsylvania 19004, 1 Decker Square |
| Wilmington | Delaware 19801, U.S. Customs House, 6th and King Streets |
| Baltimore | Maryland 21201, 1113 Federal Building, Hopkins Plaza |
| Clarksburg | West Virginia 26301, Lowndes Bank Building, 119 N. 3rd Street |
| Charleston | West Virginia 25301, 3410 Courthouse & Fed. Bldg., 500 Quarrier Street |
| Pittsburgh | Pennsylvania 15222, Federal Bldg., 1000 Liberty Avenue |
| Richmond | Virginia 23240, Federal Bldg., 400 N. 8th Street |
| Washington | D.C. 20417, 1405 I Street, N.W. |
| Atlanta | Georgia 30309, 1401 Peachtree St., N.E. |
| Birmingham | Alabama 35205, 908 S. 20th Street |
| Charlotte | North Carolina 28202, Addison Bldg., 222 South Church Street |
| Columbia | South Carolina 29201, 1801 Assembly Street |
| Jackson | Mississippi 39205, 245 Capitol Street |
| Gulfport | Mississippi 39501, 2500 14th Street |
| Jacksonville | Florida 32202, Federal Office Bldg., 400 W. Bay Street |
| Louisville | Kentucky 40202, Federal Office Bldg., 600 Federal Place |
| Miami | Florida 33130, Federal Building, 51 S.W. 1st Avenue |

| | |
|---|---|
| Tampa | Florida 33602, Federal Building, 500 Zack Street |
| Nashville | Tennessee 37219, 500 Union Street |
| Knoxville | Tennessee 37902, 502 South Gay Street |
| Memphis | Tennessee 38103, Federal Building, 167 No. Main Street |
| Chicago | Illinois 60604, Federal Office Bldg., 219 So. Dearborn Street |
| Springfield | Illinois 62701, 502 Monroe Street |
| Cleveland | Ohio 44199, 1240 E. 9th Street |
| Columbus | Ohio 43215, 50 West Gay Street |
| Cincinnati | Ohio 45202, 5026 Federal Building, 550 Main Street |
| Detroit | Michigan 48226, 1249 Washington Boulevard |
| Marquette | Michigan 49855, 502 West Kaye Avenue |
| Indianapolis | Indiana 46204, 36 South Pennsylvania Street |
| Madison | Wisconsin 53703, 25 West Main Street |
| Milwaukee | Wisconsin 53203, 238 W. Wisconsin Avenue |
| Eau Claire | Wisconsin 54701, 510 So. Barstow Street |
| Minneapolis | Minnesota 55402, 816 2nd Ave. South |
| Dallas | Texas 75202, 1309 Main Street |
| Albuquerque | New Mexico 87101, Fed. Bldg., 500 Gold Ave., S.W. |
| Los Cruces | New Mexico 88001, 1015 El Paso Road |
| Houston | Texas 77002, 808 Travis Street |
| Little Rock | Arkansas 72201, 377 P.O. & Courthouse Bldg., 600 W. Capitol Avenue |
| Lubbock | Texas 79408, Federal Office Building, 1616 19th Street |
| El Paso | Texas 79901, 109 N. Oregon Street |
| Marshall | Texas 75670, 505 East Travis Street |
| New Orleans | Louisiana 70130, 124 Camp Street |
| Oklahoma City | Oklahoma 73102, 30 N. Hudson Street |
| San Antonio | Texas 78205, 301 Broadway |
| Lower Rio Grande Valley | Harlingen, Texas 78550, 219 E. Jackson Street |
| Corpus Christi | Texas 78401, Post Office & Custom House Building |
| Kansas City | Missouri 64106, 911 Walnut Street |
| Des Moines | Iowa 50309, New Federal Bldg., 210 Walnut Street |
| Omaha | Nebraska 68102, Federal Bldg., 215 N. 17th Street |
| St. Louis | Missouri 63102, Federal Bldg., 210 North 12th Street |
| Wichita | Kansas 67202, 120 South Market Street |
| Denver | Colorado 80202, 721 19th Street |
| Casper | Wyoming 82601, 300 North Center Street |
| Fargo | North Dakota 58102, 653 2nd Avenue, North |

| | |
|---|---|
| Helena | Montana 59601, Power Block Bldg., Main & 6th Avenue |
| Salt Lake City | Utah 84111, 22 Federal Building, 125 So. State Street |
| Sioux Falls | South Dakota 57102, National Bank Bldg., 8th and Main Avenue |
| San Francisco | California 94102, Federal Bldg., 450 Golden Gate Avenue |
| Fresno | California 93721, Federal Bldg., 1130 O Street |
| Honolulu | Hawaii 96813, 1149 Bethel Street |
| Agana | Guam 96910, Ada Plaza Center Building |
| Los Angeles | California 90014, 849 South Broadway |
| Las Vegas | Nevada 89101, 300 Las Vegas Blvd., South |
| San Bernardino | California 92401, 532 North Mountain Avenue |
| Phoenix | Arizona 85004, 122 N. Central Avenue |
| Tucson | Arizona 85701, Federal Bldg., 155 East Alamenda Street |
| San Diego | California 92101, 110 West C Street |
| Seattle | Washington 98104, 506 Second Avenue |
| Anchorage | Alaska 99501, 1016 West Sixth Avenue |
| Fairbanks | Alaska 99701, 510 Third Avenue |
| Juneau | Alaska 99801, Federal Building |
| Boise | Idaho 83702, 216 North 8th Street |
| Portland | Oregon 97205, 921 S.W. Washington Street |
| Spokane | Washington 99210, Courthouse Bldg., Room 651 |

You might also want to read my book *How to Make a Big Fortune As a Licensing Agent,* published by IWS, Inc., P.O. Box 186, Merrick, N.Y. 11566. The price is $15, and you should earn at least twenty times that amount from the first licensing deal you negotiate. "How can that be?" you ask.

Well, a typical license royalty is 5 percent of the product selling price. Thus, on an item selling for $1,000, the license royalty would be 0.05 ($1,000) = $50. As a license agent working on a percent-of-royalty basis, you might receive 1 percent of the selling price, or 0.01 ($1,000) = $10. On a sale of 50 items, your fee would be $10 (50 items) = $500.

Now don't let the $1,000 selling price scare you. Most licensing deals are for industrial equipment. With such products, a $1,000 selling price is like a dollar to the average person. Many industrial equipment sales deals are for $1-million, or more. Your royalty on such sales will keep you in your favorite refreshment for as long as you want, plus plenty of other goodies!

### Look at our great big world

Licensing is only one of thousands of profitable, easy-to-run businesses that can make you rich in just a few years, no matter where you live and work. Remember, good friend, there's a great big world outside your front door. Recognize how big this world is and you'll get some idea of how many chances there are for *you* to build great wealth fast. I try to show you thousands of these chances in this book.

With billions of people in the world, and millions more being added each year, your chances of hitting the BIG MONEY become *greater every* day. And, as George Eliot once said: "It is *never* too late to be or do what might have been." What this means is that you *can* do, or become, what you've always wanted to do, or become. To achieve your goals you must:

- Know what you want
- Decide how you'll get it
- Plan a course of action
- Set target dates
- Put your plan to work
- Check your progress
- Take action to improve results
- Keep pushing until you reach your goals

This book shows you exactly how to take each of these steps and achieve your money goals.

### Think wealth success to build success

You can be as successful as you want to be—if you think of yourself as being successful. Once you know what you want, take three minutes a day to think:

- How you'll use your profits
- What you'll do for other people
- Where you'll spend your time

- When you'll reach your goal
- Why you want to be a big success

These three-minute wealth-success conditioning sessions with yourself will put you in a positive frame of mind every day of the year. With a "go" situation inside your head, you'll soon find that in the outside world of work and play:

- Your work is easier
- You act faster
- Actions replace dreams
- You become more enthusiastic
- You become a vibrant, interesting person
- You make wealth success your "thing"

To keep your enthusiasm and wealth success drive in high gear *every* day of the year, I suggest that you read the monthly newsletter *International Wealth Success.* This helpful and profit-laden newsletter will, twelve times a year, give you

- Hot new ideas for earning *your* fortune
- Names and addresses for 100% financing of deals
- Numerous zero-cash business leads
- 100 percent financing of real estate and businesses
- Finder-fee leads and deals
- Financial-broker offerings
- Lenders offering millions in loans
- Export-import needs
- Hundreds of products wanted
- Licensing-agent opportunities
- Plus much more

To subscribe to this excellent newsletter for one year, send $24 to IWS Inc., P.O. Box 186, Merrick, N.Y. 11566. The monthly flow of ideas, sources, and encouragement which you receive will put many times this amount in your pocket!

## Develop a rich mental attitude

Think poor, stay poor. *Think rich, grow rich.* Life is as simple as these eight magic words. Throw the first four words out of your life by developing a *Rich Mental Attitude* (RMA) and you'll get whatever you seek in life!

No one who ever "thought poor" all his life ever grew rich. *You can't grow rich in spite of yourself!* You *must* cooperate with riches by:

- Thinking of your future *wealth*
- Recognizing that you're *entitled* to riches
- Planning how you'll *build* wealth
- Acting on your plan

As I often tell BWB's, "I've never seen a dollar bill chasing a BWB down the street." Instead, *you* must chase the money if you want to build great riches. There simply is *no* other way to get into the big time.

Now your style—that is, the way *you* chase riches—may be different from that of other BWB's. Fine! *Your style is you.* But no matter what style you select, be it:

- Relaxed, easy-going
- Intense, quick
- Aggressive, hard
- Smooth, oily
- Dedicated, quiet
- Enthusiastic, loud

*you* must chase the money. Recognize this truth here and now and I guarantee that you'll hit the big money within three years from today—if you work towards your goal.

So remember this simple slogan: *Think rich, be rich.* Think rich every day of your life and you'll soon wonder how you ever thought differently. The building of great wealth quickly is 90 percent a mental job and 10 percent a physical job. By thinking rich, you get 90 percent of your work done without getting out of your easy chair or your hammock! Can you think of any easier way to get rich?

So let's turn now to the job of making *you* rich anywhere in the world. I think you'll find this a delightful task full of adventure, challenges, and, best of all, rich rewards! Let's start—right now.

## POINTS TO REMEMBER

- You can get rich anywhere in the world today
- Know and use your fortune-building assets
- Resolve today to take action for your future wealth
- Build your money drive now
- Go the Golden Idea Route to your wealth
- Think success to build *your* success
- Develop a Rich Mental Attitude (RMA)
- Think rich, be rich. Think poor, be poor!

# 2

# Mail Your Way to Enormous Wealth

To begin our journey toward *your* great wealth, let's start with the easiest way for you to make it big—*mail sales.* "Why should we start with mail sales?" you ask. There are any number of reasons, but the most important ones are that a mail-sales business:

- Requires only a few dollars to start
- Can be run in your spare time
- Can be run in your home—anywhere
- Is highly profitable
- Has very low costs
- Requires very few workers
- Is quickly expandable

Lastly, firms I'm associated with have sold many millions of dollars worth of products through mail order and direct mail. Since I've been closely involved with these sales, I've learned a little about the art of profitable mail selling which I want to pass on to you. So let's see if we can put *you* into this exciting and rewarding business of selling by mail anywhere in the world.

**Get your terms straight**

As our first step in putting you into mail sales, let's define what we mean by the various terms you'll use in mail selling. You'll

36

profit enormously if you keep these definitions in mind as you read this chapter.

> *Mail order* is the selling of products or services by the use of ads in magazines, newspapers, and other publications, with the buyer sending his order and money by mail.
> *Direct mail* is the selling of products or services by the use of ads which are sent through the mail to prospective customers, and the customer places his order by returning a coupon and money in the mail. Sometimes he returns only the coupon and he's billed later.
> *Mail selling* is the use of either or both mail order and direct mail to sell products or services. Today some people call mail selling direct marketing.

### Mail selling—the wave of the future

At the time of this writing, a survey by a major consulting firm showed that the total cost of one visit by an industrial salesman to a customer or prospect in his territory was $43.35! Yet I remember—not so long ago—when we thought that a cost-per-visit by a salesman of $20 was enormous. Thus, the cost of sales calls has more than doubled in just a few years. And do you know what, friend? The cost of making personal sales visits will double again in the next several years!

What's one answer to the skyrocketing cost of sales visits? One very efficient answer is *mail selling.*

"But postage, printing, and labor costs are rising too," you say. That's true. But surveys and studies show that it will *always* be cheaper to sell by mail than by personal visits by a salesman. Also, postage costs will *never* rise to the level where one letter costs close to $50 to mail!

Mail selling has many other advantages, including:

- Easy repeating of the offer
- Many messages in one "call"
- Convenience for both buyer and seller
- Fully traceable results
- Easy testing of different offers
- Low cost

So if you want to get in on the selling wave of the future, be sure to consider mail order and direct mail. You will never regret going into mail selling because each sales effort will teach you something new about this wonderful way of doing business that you can do:

- From your home
- At the nearest mail box
- Without personal sales calls
- With numerous products

## How to make a million in mail selling

Yes, you *can* make a million in mail order and direct mail if:

- You *learn* all about the business
- You *follow* the advice of the pros
- You *test* each sales campaign
- You *keep* an eye on the competition
- You *search* daily for new items to sell

Let's take a quick look at each of these items. Such a look should help you decide if mail selling is the best business for you.

### LEARN ALL ABOUT MAIL SELLING

Many people dream of starting a mail-order and direct–mail business on their kitchen table. "All you have to do is address the envelopes and send them out," one such BWB told me recently. Friends, I *wish* mail selling were that easy. But, I'm sorry to say, it isn't.

To be successful in any business you *must* know the basic methods and procedures of the business. Without this know-how you can make serious mistakes which might:

- Delay your rise to a great fortune
- Cause you to lose money
- Get you into legal problems

To learn about mail order and direct mail as a business, I suggest that you (1) read these *FREE* booklets:

## FROM THE SMALL BUSINESS ADMINISTRATION

### Free management aids

Analyzing Your Cost of Marketing, #85
Profile Your Customers to Expand Sales, #192
Marketing Planning Guidelines, #194

### Free marketers' aids

Checklist for Going Into Business, #71
Checklist for Successful Retail Advertising, #96

### Free business bibliographies

Selling by Mail Order, #3
Marketing Research Procedures, #9

(To order any of the above booklets, see the instructions in Chapter 1 of this book.)

(2) Attend a course on the subject in a school, usually a university or a college, or (3) take one of the self-study courses given by various firms and schools. The best such self-study course I know of is the *Mail Order Riches Program* available for $99.50 from IWS Inc., P.O. Box 186, Merrick, N.Y. 11566. This *Program* will give you an excellent basic education in mail order and direct mail. It should also prevent you from running into the problems mentioned earlier.

## FOLLOW THE ADVICE OF MAIL-ORDER PROS

Mail order and direct mail have a long and successful sales history, particularly in the United States and, more recently, in Europe. Many BWB's have made their first million in mail selling quickly and easily.

Out of this long history has grown a body of rules, findings, and useful methods. Many of these (in fact *all* you need as a beginner) are given in the *Mail Order Riches Program* mentioned before.

When you study this *Program,* or that of any other mail-sales professional, you may find that you don't agree with all the advice given. Fine! This means that you're thinking. But let me say this:

> Try the advice of the pros before tossing it out. You'll usually find that, in the main, the advice of the pros is valid and accurate.

As your mail sales business grows you can begin to draw some conclusions based on your own experience. Then you, too, can give advice to beginners to help them get started! You might even start your own mail sales school or course.

## TESTING IS ANOTHER WORD FOR SUCCESS

Some BWB's think that all you need do in direct mail is send out 100, 1,000, or 5,000 letters to any list of names and you'll make a pile of money. This just isn't so. You must *test* each list before you mail across it, as mail-order operators say. "How do I test?" you ask.

You test a list by mailing to only part of it—say 10 percent of the total. You have the test names picked at random so the results you get are typical of the entire list.

Any direct-mail testing you do should be guided by the long experience of many pros who say:

> Aim at a 3-for-1 return from every direct-mail test. Do not extend the mailing if your return is under 3-for-1.

Now don't let the 3-for-1 throw you. It simply means your finances work out as follows for any successful direct-mail test or campaign:

| Cost of Mailing | Value of Sales Made |
|---|---|
| $ 100 | $ 300 |
| 200 | 600 |

| Cost of Mailing | Value of Sales Made |
|---|---|
| $ 300 | $ 900 |
| 400 | 1,200 |
| 500 | 1,500 |
| 1,000 | 3,000 |
| 5,000 | 15,000 |
| 10,000 | 30,000 |
| x | 3x |

So you see, all you need do is multiply your mailing cost by three. Your mailing cost includes the following for your direct-mail advertising pieces:

- Postage
- Printing
- Labor
- Envelopes
- Addressing

Note that your mailing cost does *not* include the:

- Cost of the product sold
- Product shipping cost
- Overhead—rent, light, heat, and so forth
- Your profit

These costs come out of the $3 you get from every $1 you spend for direct mail.

If you want to earn *profits*—which is the name of this mail-sales game—you *must* test each offer you plan. Your test can be made so you offer different:

- Prices
- Terms
- Features
- Payment plans
- Advertising copy

To find out what results different tests give you, use a form like Figure 2-1. With this form on hand, you can easily determine which offer "pulled" the best—that is, which offer generated the largest sale. To get dependable results from your direct-mail tests:

Change only one item (such as price) at a time. Then you will know what produced the larger (or smaller) sale.

### MAIL TEST RESULTS

| Test No. | 1 | 2 |
|---|---|---|
| Name of List | Mail-order buyers | Auto owners |
| Number Mailed | 10,000 | 10,000 |
| Cost of Mailing, $ | 1,000 | 1,000 |
| Sales Made, $ | 2,231 | 3,039 |
| Sales/Cost Ratio | 2.231 | 3.039 |

Figure 2-1

Without this *single-variable* approach, you will have trouble getting accurate results from your tests. Why? Because if you change more than one item at a time—such as price and payment terms—you won't know which was the cause of your sales rise or fall. So take my advice because I've worked with this approach in helping people profitably sell some $150-million worth of products by mail.

### Keep your eye on the competition

Mail selling is a great game of follow-the-leader. For example, let's say that you're an expert accountant and that you decide to sell by mail a series of correspondence courses in accounting for small businessmen. (This, incidentally, isn't a bad idea for a profitable business!)

You study the market carefully to learn:

- How many small businessmen there are
- What publications they read
- Who rents mailing lists of small businessmen
- How much businessmen might pay for such a course

Your findings show that there is a large market for one such course at a price of $199.50. So you decide to run a few test ads for your course. You pick three monthly magazines which your market study shows are read by small businessmen. Your ads run two months after you place them. (It usually takes about this long to get an ad in a monthly magazine.)

Orders pour into your mailbox. You're delighted, particularly since so many people pay cash ($199.50) with their order. You begin your course and soon you're getting complimentary letters telling you how good your lessons are. You expand your ad spending and take space in a dozen magazines. You also begin to do some direct mail—after your tests of various lists that you rent from list brokers show a better than 3-for-1 response.

Money pours into your mailbox every day of the week. Soon your total income before expenses is $5,000 per week. Why are you so successful? Because you:

- Started with a good idea
- Tested your idea
- Used your test results
- Pushed ahead with your idea

You're very happy and you look ahead to a bright future, using the correspondence course approach to teach small businessmen various subjects.

### Every business has its problems

But six months after you start your business you get a terrible shock. Glancing through one of the magazines in which you advertise, you see an ad for a course that's almost an exact copy of yours. "They can't do this to me," you shout. "I'll sue!"

After a few days you calm down, particularly when you see other ads for courses competing with *your* competitors.

What you're seeing at work is the imitation of a successful idea, a common occurrence in mail selling. People imitate because:

- It's easier to imitate than to innovate
- People, in general, dislike thinking
- If you're making money from the idea, so can they
- Good ideas are scarce

But don't worry too much about the imitation of your idea. If you reached the market first, you can probably beat out the latecomers because you can:

- Come up with new ideas
- Apply your test data
- Build your reputation by claiming that you're the first, largest, best, and so forth.

Competition, in general, is good for your business, and for you personally because it:

- Keeps you alert
- Gives you ideas
- Keeps your message before the public

## Learn from your competition

Your competition learned from you—in fact, some people might say they *stole* your idea from you! Now I'm *not* recommending that you steal ideas from others. But I am recommending that you *learn* from your competition.

Work on the ideas you get from your competition and make those ideas better. This is called *innovative imitation.* I personally know folks who, using this technique, have sold more than a million dollars worth of products based on just *one* mail-selling idea! And friend, if these folks can do it, *you* can, too. Why? Because they weren't even smart enough to read a book on making big money until *after* they became successful!

Why is innovative imitation important to you? Because, by using this technique you can:

- Let your competition do the research
- Profit from the mistakes of others
- Make money faster
- Run fewer risks
- Expand your business faster

## How to keep up with competition

To learn from your competition and keep up with the new items they introduce, take these six steps:

1. Read the important magazines and newspapers in your field.
2. Clip key articles, ads, new-product releases.
3. Note exactly what new offers your competition is making.
4. Decide if a similar offer, with suitable improvement made by you, would be bought by *your* customers.
5. Test the offer if you think your customers would buy it.
6. Expand to full scale if your tests are successful.

If I can offer you any warning on innovative imitation, it is this:

> Don't rush into a new line or improvement every time a competitor does. In many cases, your competitor may just be testing the market. Watch his ads for at least six months before going ahead with your offer.

Set some innovative-imitation time goals for *your* mail selling business and the products you are offering. Typical time goals which you might use *before* you will make a similar, but improved, offer are:

| TYPE OF PRODUCT | TIME GOAL FOR ME |
|---|---|
| 1. Novelties for general public | 3 months |
| 2. Correspondence courses | 12 months |
| 3. Books, publications | 18 months |
| 4. Tools, specialty items | 12 months |
| 5. Franchises | 24 months |
| 6. Personal advice, consultation | 12 months |

Using these, or similar, time goals will keep you from:

- Imitating a failure
- Losing money by too-early spending
- Acting from hysteria instead of thought

Now for an important word of caution to you. Whenever you develop a new or revised product or service based in part on another product or service be sure you:

- Do not infringe on any patents, copyrights, or licenses
- Add a genuine improvement, instead of just copying someone else's ideas
- Put *your* ideas into the product or service
- Consult an attorney familiar with your business *before* you introduce a new product or service

By following the above hints you should be able to avoid most problems. Just be sure to know what you're doing at all times!

### Advertise your way to wealth

In mail selling you'll advertise in either, or both, of two ways:

(1) Space and/or classified ads in magazines, newspapers, etc.
(2) Direct-mail ads to customers and potential customers

Let's look at both types of advertising to see how you can fit them into your wealth plans. In showing you how to build your fortune anywhere in the world using mail selling, I'll show you, and talk about, a number of ad campaigns I'm familiar with. Since I know exactly how much money each ad campaign brought in (a statistic which is very difficult to get in any business), I can show *you* how to get richer, faster.

### Consider space ads for your product

You probably will run *space ads,* Figure 2-2, for your product sooner or later. But you might wish to start with, or also use, *classified ads,* Figure 2-3. "What's the difference between these two types of ads?" you ask.

There are a number of differences between space and classified ads, including:

- Space ads can use illustrations; classified ads *usually* cannot.

# *INTERNATIONAL WEALTH SUCCESS,* INC

## THE WORLD-WIDE MONTHLY NEWSLETTER OF UNUSUAL
## BUSINESS OPPORTUNITIES FOR WEALTH BUILDERS

Twelve **BIG** issues each year bring you profitable money-making ideas you can use anywhere, any time. Here are a few ways you are shown to help you on your path to **GREAT** riches:

- 100%, 110%, 115% FINANCING (MONEY) sources
- Compensating-balance loan sources
- NEW WEALTH IDEAS EVERY MONTH
- MANY, many sources of BUSINESS LOANS
- Part-time MONEY—MAKING IDEAS
- MAIL—ORDER RICHES opportunities
- HUNDREDS OF FINDERS FEE listings
- WORLDWIDE INTERNATIONAL MONEY—MAKING IDEAS
- Fast-fortune easy-money wealth deals
- FRANCHISE RICHES ideas and METHODS
- CAPITAL AVAILABLE FOR BORROWERS OF ALL TYPES
- Monthly TY HICKS page where TY talks to YOU
- FINANCIAL BROKER OPPORTUNITIES
- THOUSANDS of other ideas, sources and ways to EARN BIG MONEY and MAKE YOUR FORTUNE TODAY!
- WAYS TO GET MONEY YOU NEED
- UNIQUE TECHNIQUES to earn BIG MONEY
- SECRETS that PUT CASH in YOUR POCKET!

*SUBSCRIBE TODAY-- only $24 per year brings you this up-to-date NEWSLETTER.*

*ONE IDEA FROM ONE ISSUE COULD MAKE YOU WEALTHY FOREVER.*

*FILL IN THE COUPON BELOW: ENCLOSE YOUR CHECK OR MONEY ORDER NOW!*

*YOU'LL BE GLAD YOU DID. MAIL TODAY!*

$$$$$$$$$$$$$$$$$$$$$$$$$$$$$$$$$$$$$$$$$$$$$$$$$$$$$$$$$$$$$$$

INTERNATIONAL WEALTH SUCCESS, INC., P.O. BOX 186, MERRICK, N.Y. 11566

Here's my $24 for a one-year subscription to the INTERNATIONAL WEALTH SUCCESS Newsletter. Begin my subscription with the next issue.

Name_____

Address_____

City_____State_____Zip Code_____

$$$$$$$$$$$$$$$$$$$$$$$$$$$$$$$$$$$$$$$$$$$$$$$$$$$$$$$$$$$$$$$

Run FREE ADS. Send us one or more ads to be run **FREE** for you in the first issue in which space is available.

GOOD LUCK TO YOU!                                    GOOD LUCK TO YOU!

**Figure 2-2**

**Figure 2-3**

- Space ads may cost more because the minimum size allowed may be larger than the smallest classified ad.
- Space ads may have to be designed by an ad agency; classified ads are usually designed by the publication (called pub-set).
- Space ads can be located almost anywhere in a publication; classified ads usually must run in the classified-ad columns.
- Space ads may generate larger sales than classified ads, but the reverse may also be true for some products.

Now here are some questions and answers on space ads which will help you understand them better.

*Q*. When should I use space ads?

*A*. Space ads should be used when you:

- Need large paper areas to show your product or idea
- Want to impress potential customers
- Seek to attract instant attention
- Have a long message for your potential customers

*Q*. Why should I use space ads?

*A*. Space ads give you the only means for obtaining page space in a magazine or newspaper other than by classified ads or editorial coverage. Since editorial coverage is free, you are limited in the amount you can get in one publication. However, there is almost no restriction on the amount of advertising space you can obtain—other than the money you have available to pay for it, and the amount of space that is worthwhile for one or more products.

*Q*. Should I *always* use space ads?

*A*. No! Many times your product or service can best be sold by classified ads, or by direct mail. The only way to determine which is best for you and your product is by testing.

## Try classified ads for your mail selling

Classified ads, Figure 2-3, usually cost less than space ads. And some classified ads can really pull in the money for you. Thus, one famous classified ad, which you may have seen, has pulled $5-million worth of business in 30 years. During that time, the ad cost some $300,000 to run. Thus, it pulled in more than sixteen times its cost! This advertiser *really* got his 3-for-1.

As a start, I recommend that you consider using classified ads because they are cheaper and quicker to run than the usual space ad. Incidentally, all the products covered in the ads in Figures 2-2 and 2-3 are available today in their newest editions and are selling extremely well. But before you spend money on classified ads for your products I recommend that you consider ways by which you can obtain free editorial space for your products or services.

## Get free editorial space for your items

Editorial space is that part of a publication in which the articles, stories, and news items appear. It's the part of a publication that the editors put together. The other part of the usual publication is, of course, the advertising space, which includes the classified columns.

You can get plenty of free editorial space for your mail-sales products and services. All you need is a:

- Typewriter
- Supply of paper
- Roll of stamps
- List of suitable publications

Now I'd like to show you how to use these, based on my experience. During my early career I spent some seven years on the editorial staff of one of America's largest magazines. For several years I edited the new-product columns of the magazine and handled thousands of these items. Here's how to prepare a new-product release that delights an editor and makes you rich.

(As an aside, just remember that editorial space can be as valuable as, or perhaps more valuable than, advertising space. So if you get a full-page write-up for your product in a publication that is charging $5,000 per page for advertising—and that is a low page rate these days—you've obtained $5,000 worth of free ads for nothing more than a stamp and some time!)

## How to prepare releases that get published

Here are five helpful steps for preparing news releases that can make you a rich mail-sales tycoon. Follow these rules and you can break into print in just a few weeks.

(1) Type every news release. This is a positive *must!* Never submit a handwritten or handprinted release—you're just wasting your time and the editor's.
(2) Use the standard news-release layout. An 8 1/2 x 11 inch typed page is good for a profit-generating news release.
(3) Type your news release double space. The editor frequently edits your news release by hand and he needs the double-spacing for that purpose.
(4) Send your release to *every* important local, national, and international magazine, newspaper, and journal in your field. Your cost is just pennies but the publicity you obtain can be worth thousands of dollars.
(5) Keep a steady flow of releases on *new* and markedly improved products or services in the mail. With such an approach you are bound to hit the publicity jackpot sooner than you think.

## Where to find publicity outlets

For your local area, you are probably better informed than anyone as to the names and locations of:

- Small newspapers
- Local magazines

- Association journals
- Religious publications

Send releases to all these outlets. It costs you only a stamp.

When you go national, refer to copies of *Standard Rate and Data* in your local library. This monthly publication has editions covering popular magazines, trade magazines, and newspapers. Address your publicity release thus:

News Editor or New-Products Editor
Name of Publication
Address of Publication

depending on whether you are promoting a new or improved service (News Editor) or product (New-Products Editor). For the names of overseas magazines and newspapers, refer to a copy of *Newspaper Rates and Data,* published by Standard Rate and Data, and available in large local libraries.

## Make it big in mail sales on pennies

For your first news release, save yourself some money and have it printed in black and white. This is the cheapest way. Going to one or more colors won't get you any additional publicity but it *will* cost you more money. Typical prices of 100 copies of black on white releases offset printed are:

100 copies, $1.95 to $3.95
Additional 100 copies, 50¢ per 100

The lower, $1.95, price is that charged by printers hungry to get your business, while the $3.95 price is typical of franchised "instant" printers in small cities. Either way, the cost is nominal. You must supply *camera-ready* copy, that is, a page which is ready to be photographed by the printer.

To make millions from pennies in mail selling, take these steps:

(1) Have your news release printed—*include in the release the price of your product or service.*
(2) If you are promoting a product, have a photograph of it made.
(3) Have the photograph printed. Use black and white—few publications can handle color.

(4) Choose suitable magazines and newspapers for running your release.

(5) Send the release by first-class mail to the publications you've chosen—remember that the more releases you send out, the larger the number of publications that will run it. Include the photo with the release.

(6) Fill orders for which you receive payment from readers of the releases.

(7) Build a mailing list of your customers.

(8) Develop new, related products or services, to sell to your mailing list.

The key to making profit from the publicity you obtain from product and news releases is:

> Always include the price of your product or service in the release so that prospective customers can order directly from the published release.

By including your price in your news or product release you give your customer the opportunity to order on impulse. With a good product or service available, I'm sure that your experience will duplicate mine, namely that:

> Impulse buying of items listed or described in editorial columns is more common than most people realize. Such buying can be profitable sales to you and can put you on the road to great wealth.

Now let me give you some golden hints on ways for keeping every customer happy in your mail selling activities. Here they are.

## Make life easier for your customers

The life of any consumer isn't easy these days. We all know the problems that consumers—yes, you and I and the rest of the civilized world—face, namely:

- High prices
- Lower quality

- Slow delivery
- Excessive ad claims
- Poor service
- Difficult communication

To reduce such problems in *your* mail selling business:

(1) Be completely *honest* at all times
(2) Send out products quickly
(3) Refund money to unhappy customers
(4) Keep product quality high
(5) Charge fair prices
(6) Answer letters your customers write to you

## How mail selling can make your fortune

You *can* make a million in mail sales anywhere in the world. But I must level with you and tell you that making a fortune in mail selling takes more these days than addressing mail on the kitchen table. You have to approach your business in a more planned manner. This chapter outlines the steps you should consider taking. Then you can duplicate the fast mail sales fortunes made by beginners who have had good training such as that given by the IWS *Mail-Order Riches Program* and other good courses on mail sales.

### A MILLION UNITS BY MAIL

When miniskirts and other short, youthful fashions hit the world, ladies needed more than just stockings to wear under the new styles. That's when pantyhose became popular with women everywhere.

Tom L., a BWB who keeps alert to new developments, noticed how pantyhose became instant hits with the gals in his family. Though these gals loved their pantyhose, they did complain about the prices they had to pay—anywhere from $4 to $6 per pair. This made Tom think. If he could only find a maker of pantyhose who could make the product cheaply enough to sell at $1.00 per pair, Tom thought, he could make a fortune for both the manufacturer *and* himself selling the product by mail to women throughout the world.

Then, by great luck, Tom saw an item in the *Worldwide Riches Opportunities* which listed an overseas manufacturer seeking an American outlet for his superior pantyhose, which could sell for $1 per pair. Tom wrote the firm and quickly arranged a suitable deal to import (see Chapter 6) the pantyhose on a trial basis.

Next came a mailing list. After thinking it over, Tom decided that the expense of mailing-list rental was too great to justify the cost. So he used third class mail addressed to "Occupant" at a specified address. Tom's reasoning was that almost every home had one or more gals interested in buying superior pantyhose at reduced cost. To simplify his activities, Tom asked his customers to:

(a) Pay cash with their order
(b) Order six pairs at a time
(c) Choose no more than two colors

Tom's first mailing to 10,000 local homes generated 500 orders—a fantastic return of 5 percent. Tom was off and running. Using this technique of occupant mailing—sometimes called *junk mail* (which it really isn't)—Tom has sold several million dozen pairs of pantyhose. He's now expanding his coverage to other products and is also renting his mailing list for extra income. Today Tom is a pantyhose millionaire—all by mail selling!

## SELL FRANCHISES BY MAIL

Most mail sales businesses sell a product of some kind such as an auto accessory or part, a tool, a book, the pantyhose mentioned above, and so on. Many fortunes have been, and are being, made from the mail sales of one or more products.

Al Q. knew this when he decided to try mail selling as a way to build a fast fortune. But instead of trying to sell a product, Al decided to try a "paper" business, that is, a business having no product other than print on paper. Such a business has many advantages, including:

• Small capital to start
• No large factory needed
• Small payroll
• Low inventory

In searching around for a good paper business, Al came across the authoritative *Franchise Riches Program: A Complete Guide to Becoming a Successful Franchisor.* This *Program* intrigued Al because it showed him exactly how to be a franchisor, that is, how to *sell* franchises for $1,000 to $50,000, or more, in *his* business. It is the only

*Program,* course, or other instruction (that I know of) available anywhere in the world that shows you how to *collect* money in franchising instead of paying it out. Yet the Program costs only $99.50 and is available from IWS Inc., P.O. Box 186, Merrick, N.Y. 11566.

Al bought the *Franchise Riches Program* and studied it. With the information he got from the Program, Al picked a fire-extinguisher sales franchise to market by mail. And instead of going to men to sell his franchise to, Al decided to try to sell to housewives. Why? Because housewives are:

- Safety conscious
- Willing to work for less
- In need of extra money
- Usually bored with housework
- Ambitious
- Ready to sell good products

To build a large sales force, Al decided to keep his franchise fee low—$250. But to increase his income, Al arranged to be paid a commission on all sales his franchisees made. This commission would be paid to Al by the fire extinguisher company whose products his franchisees would sell. It was easy to arrange a deal for a 12 percent commission because all firms, everywhere, want to increase their sales. And they're delighted to pay a commission to anyone who can increase their sales!

Al decided to sell his franchise by mail in several ways, namely:

- Direct mail to ladies' clubs
- "Occupant" mail to homes
- Classified ads in shelter magazines
- Direct mail to adult education groups

Starting with the ladies' clubs, Al was astounded by the results. He received forty franchise payments for the first 1,000 ads mailed. This is a return of 4 percent—very high for this type of mailing.

With the $10,000 he received from his first mail sales, Al expanded his coverage. Soon he had 200 payments for franchises in the till.

With business booming, Al decided to raise the price of his franchise to $2,500. And do you know what happened? Business hardly fell off at all! This brings out an important concept, namely:

Be careful not to underprice a good franchise offer. Figure the income your franchisees can earn and price accordingly.

Today Al is netting over $200,000 a year from his franchise business and related commissions. Yet he is using the cheapest method of sales known today—mail selling—the wave of the future!

### Go get your wealth—today

You now know the basics of mail selling. By using the various ideas and aids given in this chapter, you should easily be able to:

- Get started in mail selling
- Build your income
- Expand to great wealth

And, as a final thought, keep in mind the following about mail selling:

- It's the wave of the future
- Is bound to grow
- Can be conducted from any location
- Is highly profitable
- May make you a fortune

Truly, friend, mail selling is one of the best businesses around. I know because I've been in on the selling of some $150-million of products by mail during my business career. To me, it's one of the better ways for *you* to get richer, sooner. Try it and see for yourself!

### POINTS TO REMEMBER

- Mail selling can put you into the big money.
- Train yourself for mail selling by taking one of the better courses on the subject.
- Take the advice of mail-order pros, if you're just starting.
- TEST, Test, is the inflexible rule of making money in mail selling. Testing is another word for success.
- Aim at 3-for-1 returns on all direct-mail sales.
- Know when to imitate and when to innovate.
- Use ads and publicity to build your sales.

# 3

# Go International to Collect
# Your Mail Riches

When I talk to Beginning Wealth Builders (BWB's) around the world, I like to tell them to use my 3M formula for getting rich, namely: *Make Mail Millions.* For truly, good friend, *you* can make your fortune in mail selling today easier, sooner, and better than in almost any other business, IF YOU USE THE RIGHT APPROACH. In this book I give you the approach that has worked for thousands of successful, happy BWB's.

### Go international with your mail sales

No matter where you live you can sell the products of your country in another country by putting the power of the mails to work alongside carefully chosen classified or space ads. How can I say this? Because, friend, I have operated an international mail sales business for years, selling products throughout the world. Also, a number of my friends make big money the same way.

"But what about postage?" you ask. "The postage bill will kill me!" Not if you figure your postage as part of the cost of doing business. Where postage costs are excessively high in relation to your product cost, you can:

(1) Add postage costs to the product cost

(2) Show the postage cost separately and have the customer pay the postage

(3) Ship the item by surface mail at the lowest cost possible

Now, let's say that I've convinced *you* that international mail sales might be for you. How can you get started? Here's how, in eight easy, fast steps.

### Pick your overseas-sale product

People overseas need different products, in many cases, from customers in domestic markets. Thus, a good friend of mine has a very profitable and fast-growing business selling thousands of technical books which he markets by overseas mail sales. Are these the recently published or newer books? No! They are old books— that were published 25 to 50 years ago.

"How can he sell such old stuff?" you ask. "Very easily," I reply. "Many overseas countries—such as the under-developed ones—are so far behind in their technology that a 25-year-old book seems brand new to them!" These "old" books are in such great demand that my friend pays finders' fees to people who find copies of old engineering books in good condition. If he can't find enough copies of a good book, he pays to have it reprinted.

When picking your overseas product, keep these important ideas in mind. Overseas people:

(a) Generally need *lower-cost* products

(b) Seek *simpler* products

(c) Will read *long* ads

(d) Are willing to wait for delivery

### Use ideas as guides

Using the above ideas as guides you can start to explore, that is, test your product choice on a dry-run basis. For instance, let's say that you see an ad for the auction of several different types of can openers, both the manual and electric types. Right away you decide that one of these might be a good product for overseas mail-order sales. So you start to explore the profit potential for yourself.

You go to your local library and get several books on the countries in which you think you can sell can openers. From a careful reading of these books you quickly learn that:

(a) The people in the countries you've been considering *don't* use canned foods because they can't afford them.
(b) No other canned goods are used in these countries.
(c) Electric can openers wouldn't sell because very few homes have electricity.

## Make research pay off

But your research isn't wasted. You learn that the people in the countries you have in mind are wild for:

- Fancy combs
- Pocket knives
- Cheap wrist watches
- Low-cost bicycles
- Small transistor radios

With this information in hand, you dry-run your market more completely. To do this, you more accurately select the countries in which you'll do overseas mail sales. Let's see how you'll do that.

## Investigate your overseas markets

To be a mail-order sales market, an overseas country must have:

- Enough people—say 100,000 or more—to make a potential market
- Demand for a product based on: (1) contact with the outside world, (2) local customs, or (3) personal habits
- Access to publications which carry mail-order ads
- Dealers interested in handling mail-order type products

To find out if the countries that interest you can meet these requirements,

(1) Check the population statistics using *The World Almanac*, the United Nations *Demographic Yearbook*, and similar publications available in your local library.
(2) Use geography and similar books, also available in most

libraries, to learn how much the people know about external products, and what local or personal customs might lead to sales of the products you're promoting.

(3) Next, chcck the international distribution of the publications in which you might advertise. You can do this by glancing at the circulation statement given in *Standard Rate and Data,* available in any large public library. If the overseas circulation is small—say only a few hundred copies—then you might want to consider using local publications published in each country instead of large international publications. This approach can considerably reduce your ad cost.

(4) Obtain a copy of Volumes 1 and 2 of *Worldwide Riches Opportunities:* 2500 Great Leads for Getting Rich in Overseas Trade Without Leaving Home, $25 per volume, from IWS Inc., P.O. Box 186, Merrick, N.Y. 11566. Check in each volume the listing of dealers, importers, wholesalers, and the like, who might handle your product in the countries that interest you. If you find several importers seeking your product, you can assume that it is worth sending letters to each importer to find out the quantities, delivery dates, and prices which interest him.

Once you have the information listed above, you can make a definite decision about each country you've considered. To show you how to do this, let me give you two examples of people who've hit it big in international mail sales.

## Make your promotion choices profitable

Ted C. wanted to go into international mail sales because he felt he had three great products—ladies' synthetic dresses, synthetic bedsheets, and men's synthetic shirts. Ted believed these products were great because he:

- Could buy rejects from a local mill
- Could repair the products easily
- Could undersell anyone in the world
- Had the latest fashions and designs

With his products tentatively chosen, Ted decided to study his markets. He chose three markets to study: Europe, Japan, and South America.

Using books at his local library, Ted found, at no expense other than his time and energy, that:

- European markets were flooded with cheap imitations of American products; these imitations were priced lower than he could price his products.
- Japan had strict import regulations that would severely limit the number of items which he could sell, thereby making his profit potential extemely small.
- South America was a booming, teeming market, hungry for synthetic-material products which were well designed and stylish.

With this information in hand, Ted turned to *Worldwide Riches Opportunities,* mentioned before. He was delighted to find lists of a number of importers seeking the products—and similar items—that he had available. And, of course, price was an important factor in the selection of these products by the overseas importers.

Next, Ted investigated the number of publications—newspapers and magazines—serving the South American market. He was pleased to find that next to the United States and Europe, South America probably has more newspapers and magazines than any other area in the world. And the rates charged for advertising in these magazines and newspapers are low, compared with the ad rates in similar publications in other populated areas.

With this information in hand, Ted took three quick steps:

(1) He contacted the importers listed in *Worldwide Riches Opportunities,* asking about their interest in his products.
(2) He ran a small ad in a well-known South American women's magazine, telling about his products and their prices.
(3) He ran a free ad in *International Wealth Success,* the monthly newsletter for beginning and experienced wealth builders, to which Ted was a regular (one year, or longer) subscriber.

To Ted's delight he was quickly flooded with orders from both importers and mail-order buyers. Today, less than a year later, Ted is shipping more than $70,000 per month worth of products to

South American importers and mail-order buyers. Since Ted's synthetic products are light in weight they are easily shipped by air. This means he gives fast, efficient service which keeps his buyers coming back, again and again.

### Earn high profits in your business

To those people who ask him about his profits, Ted replies: "My rate of profit is the highest in the mail-order sales business—25 percent before taxes." On a volume of $70,000 per month this means that Ted's profit is $17,500 per month, or $210,000 per year. That's not bad, particularly since Ted spends only two days a week on his international mail-order sales business. For the fun of it, figure his hourly before-tax profit, assuming that Ted puts in 15 hours per week on his business and works 50 weeks per year.*

### Start small—grow big, fast

Roberta L. went into international mail order sales to finance her vacation trips to foreign lands. When she started, Roberta hoped to earn about $50 per week from her business. Today, two years later, Roberta often has a $5,000 week. "It's almost unbelievable," Roberta laughs. "Sometimes I try to 'run away' from the money."

Since she wanted to use the "KISS principle"—Keep It Simple and Safe—in her business, Roberta chose to market baby toys by mail-order sales.

What Roberta likes about baby toys is that they are:

- Easy to ship
- Safe when properly chosen
- Simple to price
- Readily obtainable

"With such features," you ask, "why aren't more people in the business of international baby-toy mail-order sales?" For a simple

---

*$280 per hour.

reason. *Other people don't understand the market for baby toys* the way Roberta does. Why? Because before going into the baby toy business, Roberta did what every BWB should do, namely:

- Studied the *markets*
- Analyzed *which* toys would be popular
- Determined the acceptable *prices*
- Found low-cost suppliers
- Picked a profitable *marketing* strategy

Roberta's marketing strategy will interest you. Why? Because selling baby toys to *individual* overseas families by mail order and direct mail is a loss-type business. But you can make money selling this way to overseas:

- Department stores
- Military PX's
- Importers and agents
- Schools
- Libraries
- Hospitals

Using these markets and soft, safe toys, Roberta has a $250,000-per-year business going for herself, using international mail-order sales. Although she doesn't have to leave home to conduct this simple business, Roberta enjoys taking her vacations in the areas where her customers are located. Such vacations allow her to check up on the type of service her customers are receiving. This makes for repeat orders and higher profits. And the vacations are more enjoyable! Using these methods, you too can build a quick fortune in international mail-order sales.

### Get to know international mail

Some of the friendliest people in this world work in the post office—here in the United States, overseas in England, France, Germany, and elsewhere. How do I know? Because I've worked with many of these fine men and women in my own international mail-sale businesses. I've always found these people to be willing, interested, and helpful when approached in a polite and business-like way.

Every post office in the world has an enormous amount of *free, valuable* information available to the international mail sales BWB. To get this information all you need do is ask for it! This information covers:

- Lowest cost mailing rates
- Fastest methods of delivery
- Correct wrapping procedures
- Simple addressing methods

For instance, you can get fast, First-Class speedy delivery to Canada and Mexico of packages containing books for little more than the low-cost book rate. There are plenty of other valuable money-saving ideas waiting for you in your post office.

An interesting leaflet, "International Mail," is available free from the U.S. Postal Service. You should have it on hand if you plan on making international mailings because you can find in it almost anything you want to know about overseas mail.

One last point on any mail-order sales operation. Always get a receipt for the postage you buy. Your mailing costs for business purposes are, in general, completely deductible as a business expense on your income tax return.

## Know your overseas publications

In international mail-order sales you will, in general:

- Advertise less
- Spend less for ads
- Sell more to dealers

than in domestic mail-order sales. There are many reasons for this, including:

- Overseas customers buy more from dealers or shops
- Money isn't as readily available
- Mail order isn't known as well
- Sending overseas for a product takes energy

But don't let these facts discourage you. Recognize them and plan to earn a profit despite the problems. And remember, friend, *mail order is rapidly growing in importance throughout the world!*

Get to know the publications in each country in which you plan to promote your products by mail-order sales. Most of the large publications:

- Have advertising offices in foreign countries
- Publish English-language data on their ad rates
- Will translate your ads free of charge
- Are ready to help you in many ways
- Will send you free copies of back issues

Study the back issues of the publications you're considering. (You can get free copies of any magazine by writing to the ad manager and telling him you're thinking of advertising in it.)

Note these facts during your study:

- Types of items advertised
- Typical size of mail-order ads
- Location of the mail-order companies
- Average price of the mail-order products

See if your planned offering of a product or service falls within the ranges shown by the above study. If your product or service is priced about right, can be advertised in the space available, and is similar to other products being sold by mail order, then you can feel safe in running some test ads.

But if your product seems to fall short in one or more ways, you should investigate further before moving ahead. You can get much helpful information from:

- Ad departments of overseas magazines and newspapers
- Importers in the countries involved
- People familiar with the countries

Only if the opinions given by these people seem hopeful—and profitable—should you consider going ahead. Then rely on your own business sense. If your "gut feeling," as they say, tells you to go ahead, then do so. But if this same feeling warns you off, then turn to another product or market. But above all, don't give up!

And why do I say *don't give up?* Because:

This is a big world we live in. If you take the time to

study a market carefully after finding the right product
or service for it, you're certain to make money from
your sales.

Believe me when I tell you this. I have nothing to sell you
except *your* success. You can make big money in international
mail sales—if you carefully follow the general guides I've given you
in this chapter!

## POINTS TO REMEMBER

- International mail sales can add to your domestic profits.
- Postage costs are not too big a cost item in international mail sales.
- Check out overseas markets *before* you spend money on ads.
- Get free publicity for your products whenever you can.
- Study the facts about international mail.
- Check out overseas publications in which you can run ads.
- Never give up your search for ways to sell your products or services overseas.

# 4

# Export Your Way to Great Riches

Your world today is teeming with more than three billion people! And almost every one of these people needs certain basic items—a bed, clothing, grooming products, tools, toys, medicines, and so forth. *You* can supply many of these products from your own home while you export your way to great riches! And, as your exports gain wide acceptance, your wealth will grow because population experts are predicting that within a few years there will be over seven billion people in this world of ours!

## Take 11 lucky steps to export riches

There are 11 simple, fast, and luck-laden steps you can take to build export riches—no matter where you live. To take these lucky 11 steps you *don't* need a:

- High-cost business address
- Fancy office
- Factory
- Warehouse
- Big payroll
- Expensive machinery
- Patents or licenses
- College education

You do, however, need a few simple items. These items are:

- A typewriter (you can rent one)
- Letterheads (i.e. *printed* letter paper and envelopes)
- A mailing address (your home address is suitable)
- A pen to sign your name
- A few reference books (which are listed below)
- A telephone (though you *can* get by for awhile without one)

Now here are the 11 lucky steps I recommend that you consider taking to make BIG export riches yours quickly and easily. *You* can take these steps *now* because I've watched as hundreds of people everywhere have done just that. It makes no difference how small you are today. You can easily be *big* tomorrow if you take these 11 steps:

(1) Choose the *types* of products you'd like to export.
(2) Determine which overseas firms seek these types of products.
(3) Find those firms in your country which carry the products you've selected to export.
(4) Write the overseas firms you found in Step 2, telling them you can supply the products they need; ask them to tell you the quantities required.
(5) Ask for price quotes from the suppliers in your country once you know the quantities needed by the overseas firms.
(6) Send the price quotes to the overseas firm without identifying your supplier, unless you have the written Supplier Agreement mentioned later in this chapter; ask for a firm purchase order.
(7) Order the items from your supplier *after* you receive a firm purchase order and guarantee of payment.
(8) Where a cash down payment is required by your supplier, obtain this from the overseas purchaser.
(9) Add a suitable fee for your services.
(10) Arrange the shipment to the overseas purchaser.
(11) Collect the money due you; deduct your fee, and send the balance of the payment to your supplier.

## It's easy to start exporting

Let's look at how *you* can get started in exporting *your* way to great wealth. In doing this, we'll use the 11 lucky steps you will take—one at a time. To show you how *you* can take these steps, I'll put you into the business of exporting a certain product. Just keep in mind as you read about the steps that you're taking that these steps apply to *any* product you might select except, perhaps, guns, bombs, warships, and other arms products. However, I'm assuming that exporting such products does not interest you. By that I mean that I think you're probably more interested in products that *help* people (i.e. that are *constructive*), as opposed to *destructive* products. Now let's put *you* in the business of making your fortune in exporting. We'll begin with some definitions.

## How exporting can work for you

A firm or individual handling the export of items for other firms or individuals is called an *export management company,* when operating as a company, or an *export management agent,* when operating in the name of an individual. Since some Beginning Wealth Builders (BWB's) hesitate to spend the $5 most states require for the registration of a company, we'll assume that you plan to do business as an Export Management agent (EMA). Why? Because in many states you need not register your business when you operate it in your own name, such as:

John A. Doe
Export Management Agent
123 Any Street
Anytown, U.S.A. 000000

The above arrangement of your name and address might be useful to you when you have your letterhead printed. Or you can use other layouts that your printer might suggest.

## Tips for building your export income

As an EMA you can work in two ways, or in a combination of these ways:

(1) Buy-sell
(2) Commission on each sale

In the buy-sell arrangement you *buy* items from a domestic producer *after* you get orders from your overseas customers. The usual price you'll pay for items you export on a buy-sell basis is about 45 percent of the price you charge your overseas customer. Thus, on an item you sell to your overseas customer for $100 you'll pay the domestic manufacturer $45 for it. This means that your gross profit is $100 - 45 = $55 per item sold.

When you work on a commission basis, you will usually receive a commission of 5 percent to 20 percent of the price at which you sell the item to your overseas customer. Thus, on the above item, with a 20 percent sales commission, you would receive 0.20 ($100) = $20 per item sold. This is also your gross profit on the sale.

## Learn the numbers of exporting

"Ty," you say, "any fool would rather work on a buy-sell basis than on a commission basis for this item. He'd make more than twice as much on the buy-sell basis."

This is true, and it shows that you're thinking. But let's compare the two arrangements and see what *you* have to put up. On a buy-sell deal you must:

- *Buy* the item—that is put up *cash* for it
- Take *all* the credit *risk* (or buy insurance to protect yourself from bad credit)
- Probably have to pay an overseas representative a commission to help you handle the sale
- Wait to be paid by an overseas firm instead of by a firm in your own country

So you see, buy-sell may *appear* to pay you a higher profit. But like everything else in life, you must either:

- Risk more
- Wait longer
- Work harder
- Or take on all of these burdens

to earn the larger profit.

### Start right; build fast

Probably the easiest way to start in the export-import business is as a commission export management agent, working on a commission basis. Why do I say this? Because as a commission export management agent you:

- Need *no* capital (you don't *buy* anything)
- Can start *without* an office
- Don't need a payroll
- Can exist on plain paper and stamps

Once you make a few big commissions (some agents can earn as much as $1-million on *one* sale!), you can easily begin to work a few deals on a buy-sell basis. So don't knock commission sales— they can easily lead to greater income later on, after you've built some capital and experience. Or, if you want, you can make all your sales on a commission basis. Plenty of export management agents do, and get rich just as fast as the folks who work on a buy-sell basis!

The main point for you to keep in mind here is that you must be careful to:

- Start right
- Work hard
- Build fast

So if you have money, consider starting on a buy-sell basis. But if you're out of money, start as an export management commission agent. Either way, you'll eventually hit the *big* money.

**Choose the types of products you'd like to export**

You can export almost any type of product, from aardvarks to Zulu head dresses. The products or items you export can be:

- Manufactured
- Untreated raw materials
- Partially finished parts
- Fully packaged items
- Living or dead animals, fish, and the like
- Growing plants, trees, foods
- And so forth

As a general concept, you can say that

> If people need an item or product for any legitimate purpose, this item can be exported, unless there are government rules against its exportation.

But allow me a word of warning. Don't go into the business of exporting a certain item just because you *like* the product. Remember this key idea about any business, including exporting:

> Your liking of, or attraction to, a product does not necessarily make a profitable market for that product!

In general, the best products to start exporting are:

1. Manufactured industrial products
2. Industrial raw materials
3. Commercial products (office supplies, school furniture, and similar articles )
4. Consumer products (books, clothes, novelties, and so on)

So pick the general type of product you think you might export. In making your choice, these factors can help you:

(1) Knowledge of the product or business
(2) Special contacts in the supply or source end of the product or business

(3) Known large demand for the item, as determined in the next step you'll take, which is described for you now.

### Find out who wants what

Your export business will earn you profits because you serve a need—the need that overseas firms have for the products you offer to export. But before you can offer to export a product you must know who wants what.

The best way to learn who wants what is to read the various publications which list product needs of numerous firms overseas. To do this, I recommend that you start by reading the following *free* publications:

#### FROM THE SMALL BUSINESS ADMINISTRATION

### Free management aids

Developing a List of Prospects, #188
Profile Your Customers to Develop Sales, #192
What Is the Best Selling Price? #193
Marketing Planning Guidelines, #194
Expand Overseas Sales with Commerce Department Help, #199
Is the Independent Sales Agent for You? #200
Are Your Products and Channels Producing Sales? #203

### Free marketers' aids

A Pricing Checklist for Managers, #105
Building Good Customer Relations, #120

### Free bibliographies

Selling by Mail Order, #3
Marketing Research Procedures, #9
National Mailing-List Houses, #29
Distribution Cost Analysis, #34
(See Chapter 1 for details on ordering any of the above publications.)

Another way to learn who wants what is to use copies of *Worldwide Riches Opportunities:* 2500 Great Leads to Becoming Rich Without Leaving Your Own Home, Volumes 1 and 2, available for $25 each from IWS Inc., P.O. Box 186, Merrick, N.Y. 11566.

With these big books on your desk, you can easily find which overseas firms want what products. The books list:

- Products and services sought
- Type of price quotation wanted
- Name of individual to contact
- Name of firm
- Complete address of firm
- Overseas lenders who may finance your exports (Vol. 2)

To use these handy books, all you need do is:

(a) Look for listings in *Worldwide Riches Opportunities* of firms seeking the product or products you've decided to export.
(b) Study each listing to determine if the items sought are the ones you really want to export.
(c) Make a list of the firms you believe will buy your exports, using the *Worldwide Riches Opportunities* books as your guide.


**Learn who will supply your exports**

You now know *who wants what.* Your next step is:

> Find out which firms will supply the items you plan to export; try to find as many suppliers as possible.

To find the suppliers you seek, go to your public library and:

(a) Obtain a copy of *Thomas's Register of Manufacturers* and study its listings thoroughly. (If your library doesn't have a copy of this excellent 11-volume reference work, you can get details on ordering a set by writing to Thomas Publishing Co., 461 8th Avenue, New York, N.Y. 10001.
(b) Obtain copies, in your library, of directories of manufac-

turers and suppliers in various states. Study them for suitable sources of exports.

(c) Do the same with trade-association membership lists.

(d) Lastly, don't overlook annual issues of industrial magazines which often list manufacturer and product data. These issues are called by various names, including: *Buyer's Guide, Product Directory, Industry Survey,* and so forth.

(e) Prepare a list of the suppliers you think could meet your export needs.

## Obtain quotes from your supplier

Your copy of *Worldwide Riches Opportunities* usually tells you what quantities of various items the overseas buyer seeks or the basis of the price quotation he wants from you. With these facts in hand, you can easily obtain price and delivery schedule quotations from your prospective suppliers.

The best way to obtain valid price and delivery quotations from a supplier is to request the quotes using a *printed* letterhead. Handwritten requests for quotations will usually fail to bring any response—not even an acknowledgement. So resolve today to begin acting in a more professional way—if you've been trying to get along without letterheads. Make every quotation request on your printed letterhead!

## Get the highest discount possible

Now here's a valuable pointer that many beginners overlook. It is:

> Many suppliers give a larger discount on items purchased for export. So be sure to state on your quotation request that the item is for export only.

By using this pointer you can save your overseas buyer as much as 20 percent. Having the extra discount to work with may allow you to underbid another exporter who's trying to sell the same product to the same buyer you've located overseas.

Where you can locate more than one supplier, get at least two or more price and delivery quotes on the item you plan to export. With several quotes on hand, you:

- Can compare prices
- Can compare delivery schedules
- Can give your overseas customer the best deal
- Can give your overseas customer alternatives on price and delivery schedules, when such alternatives exist

Next make a list of the prices and delivery schedules you've received. Keep all the data related to one overseas customer in a single file folder. This will help you work more efficiently and more rapidly. Why waste time when saving it can put more money into your pocket?

**Work fast to save time**

Now here's another set of money-making tips you can put to work instantly in your export-import activities:

(a) When you're in a hurry, *telephone your suppliers* for a price and delivery schedule quotation.
(b) *Follow up* your telephone request with a written request on your printed letterhead.
(c) Never quote a price to your overseas customer until *after* you have a *written* price and delivery quotation from your supplier.
(d) To get the most out of your letterhead, use a company name that will be suitable for both domestic and foreign operations. Then identify your group, for the purposes of the quote, as *Export Division*. This will help establish the fact that you seek an export discount.

**Protect your time and energy investment**

When you expect to specialize in exporting one type of product, it might pay you to prepare, and have signed by each of your suppliers, a Supplier Agreement, mentioned earlier in this chapter. The usual Supplier Agreement is a letter which you send to one or more of your suppliers confirming several facts, namely:

(1) You discussed (usually on the phone) your finding of overseas customers for the supplier.
(2) Your supplier agreed to your finding such customers.
(3) He agreed to sell to you, for resale, certain types of products, materials, or services.
(4) A specific discount, or class of discount, was agreed upon by the supplier and yourself.
(5) All future sales of the specific item to the company or country mentioned in the agreement will earn a commission for you of a stated amount or percentage, whenever you negotiate the sale.

Here's a typical example of one form of the Supplier Agreement letter.
*Warning:* DO NOT USE THIS LETTER IN THE FORM GIVEN HERE UNTIL AFTER IT IS APPROVED BY YOUR LAWYER.

Your Letterhead<br>
Company Name<br>
Address<br>
Telephone

Mr. _____ _____
_____Corporation
_____
_____

Dear Mr. _____:

This letter confirms our recent conversation concerning the export of certain items available from _____ Corporation. In these conversations we mutually agreed that:

(1) _____ Corporation is interested in having me find, and sell to, overseas customers throughout the world (or in the following countries_____), the following products, materials or services_____

(2) _____ Corporation will sell to my firm, named above on this letterhead, the following_____

at an export discount of _____ percent, or _____ percent off the overseas list price.

(3) All future sales of the products, materials, or services mentioned in par. (2) in the geographic areas mentioned in par. (1) will be credited to my firm, whenever my firm negotiates the sale or there is a repeat order by an organization or individual whose first order we negotiated. For each such repeat sale a commission of _____ percent of the selling price will be paid to my firm.

(4) Please indicate your agreement to the above terms by signing in the space provided below and returning one copy of this letter to me for our files. The other copy is for your file.

Very truly yours,

_____

_____

Agreed:

_____              _____
Name; title                                   Date

## Contact your overseas customers

With your price and schedule quotes in hand, you are ready to contact your overseas customers. You can do this in three ways:

(1) Telephone
(2) Cable (Telex)
(3) Air mail

Air mail is the cheapest. However, you can often get faster action using cable or telephone. If you're in a hurry to make money in exporting, consider the possibility of using the telephone. But before you make an overseas phone call:

(1) Check out the phone rates with your local operator.
(2) Ask the operator what are the *cheapest* times for you to call.
(3) Determine, from *Worldwide Riches Opportunities,* if the overseas customer speaks English. (This is not always given but if a firm asks for quotes in the native language, you can assume they do *not* speak English fluently.)
(4) Try to obtain a person fluent in the language to talk for you, if you can't speak the language.
(5) Prepare a list of what you'll tell your overseas customer.
(6) Convert the prices you'll quote into marks, francs, pounds, or whatever other money units your customer might use.
(7) Prepare another list which details what information *you* want from your overseas customer.

If you follow these hints you won't lose time or money while making your overseas call. To keep track of how long you talk, buy one of those three-minute timing glasses and keep it alongside your phone.

### Be sure to get your share

Now here's a key pointer you should follow in *every* export deal:

> Never contact an overseas customer to give him a price quotation until after you've applied your export commission to the price of the item you're exporting.

The usual commission you'll earn on an export deal when acting as an export commission agent is 5 percent to 20 percent of the amount you charge your overseas customers for the items you export. The lower commission applies to higher priced items. Here is a typical scale of commissions which you might consider charging your suppliers:

| Price* You Charge Large-Volume Overseas Buyers, $ | Your Commission in Percent | $ |
|---|---|---|
| 1,000 | 10 | 100 |
| 5,000 | 10 | 500 |
| 10,000 | 10 | 1,000 |
| 50,000 | 10 | 5,000 |
| 100,000 | 8 | 8,000 |
| 200,000 | 7 | 14,000 |
| 300,000 | 6 | 18,000 |
| 500,000 | 5 | 25,000 |
| 500,001 and up | 5 | 25,000.05 and up |

If you cable or write your quote and you wish to use a foreign language you do not speak, obtain or refer to a copy of *Commercial Correspondence in Four Languages,* Hart Publishing Co., 510 Avenue of the Americas, New York, N.Y. 10036. This handy book allows you to write overseas letters in a foreign language quickly and easily in four languages—English, Spanish, French, and German.

## Make your correspondence pay off

Profit-making pointers which I've found useful in my overseas export correspondence—such as letters, memos, cables, and so forth—are:

(1) Always use air mail when writing—never send a quotation letter by surface mail.

(2) Use two languages (if possible) in your letter—English and the language of your overseas customer.

(3) Quote prices in both dollars and the local currency of your customer.

(4) Where quotes are requested on a c.i.f. basis (i.e.: c = cost; i = insurance; f = freight), get the necessary figures *before* you write.

---

*For smaller buyers you might raise your sales commission because you will usually do more work for them.

(5) Provide a return addressed (but not stamped) air-mail envelope for your customer to use. This prevents mistakes in your address and speeds his reply.
(6) Consider using a form letter, (available free from IWS), which your overseas customer can use to answer you quickly and effortlessly.

Remember this important fact about exporting products to overseas customers and you'll never go wrong:

> Successful exporting is really highly specialized mail order and direct mail. Make it easier for your customers to order and you'll earn higher profits sooner!

Now, for your final correspondence (phone, cable, or mail) export wealth-building strategies, keep these things in mind:

(1) *Never* identify the source of your export items unless your overseas customer asks you to do so, and you have the written Supplier Agreement, mentioned earlier.
(2) Be ready to reduce your commission if by doing so you sell the items at a profit.
(3) *Never* reveal your commission percentage or amount to your overseas customer. Your income for arranging the deal is none of his business!

## Order the items you plan to export

As soon as you have a valid purchase order from your overseas customer you can order the items from your suppliers. To prevent loss of your time and energy:

> Never order an item from your supplier until after you have a valid purchase order from your overseas customer.

This cautionary warning means that you must:

(1) *Never* order items from your supplier on speculation.
(2) *Never* lay out cash on a verbal order.

(3) Accept only *written* purchase orders.
(4) Use a *printed purchase order,* sold in stationery stores, to order your export items. (Purchase orders of this type are easily obtained from business printers.)

## Obtain the cash you need from overseas customers

Where you must make a cash down payment for the items you are exporting, insist that your overseas customer advance the needed amount to you. As a profit-making guide:

> Never lay out any of your cash for an overseas customer.
> You are better off losing the sale than putting up your
> own cash.

Follow this rule inflexibly until your export business becomes so large, and you know an overseas customer so well, that you can afford to take the risk of putting up the cash. But at the start you probably won't be able to afford the risk. Therefore:

(1) You must be businesslike at all times—this means getting the needed cash in *advance.*
(2) Overseas customers will respect you more when you insist on your rights.
(3) Getting the necessary cash in advance will allow you to start your export business for just the cost of printing and correspondence. This means you will need less than $100, if you buy wisely.

## Use a letter of credit

The safest way for you to get your money from your overseas buyer is for him to use a *letter of credit.* This is a letter which his bank sends to your bank guaranteeing that the purchase price of the goods will be paid to you when the goods are either:

(a) Shipped by you
(b) Received by the customer

Any shipping deal you work out with your customer should be mutually convenient.

You might also work out an in-between payment deal, such as half payment on shipment, the balance on receipt of the shipment. Since your shipment will almost always be protected by insurance, you need not worry about the loss of the other half of your money in the event the airplane crashes or the ship carrying your goods sinks.

### Consider using export agents

Another approach to getting your money from your overseas customers is to use an export agent. The export agent does several jobs for you, including:

- Checking out your overseas customer
- Arranging for letters of credit
- Processing export documents
- Collecting your money

"Why should I use an export agent when I can do all the work myself," you ask. True, you can do *all* this work by yourself. And plenty of beginning exporters do. But while you're doing *this* work, you can't be looking for new business or new customers. So you just have to make a business decision. You either:

- Spend your time on detailed paperwork
- Or pay someone else to do the paperwork

Now there is really nothing difficult about doing export-import paperwork. The book *How to Prepare and Process Export-Import Documents:* A Completely Illustrated Guide, available for $25 from IWS, Inc., tells you exactly how to handle the paperwork in exporting. But it *does* take time to do this paperwork. An export agent can save you this time because his staff will do the work for you. But you will have to pay a small fee for the work, which will reduce your profit a trifle.

## Use smart-money export methods

Two other ways to save time and effort in exporting are:

(1) Sell to local reps
(2) Sell to import agents

In the United States today, there are thousands of local representatives (reps) of overseas governments and firms. They act for:

- Military buying groups
- Civilian buying groups
- Industrial firms
- Special projects of various kinds

You can sell directly to many of these groups and bypass the filling out of export documents and long waits for your money. A comprehensive list of these reps, *Overseas Buying Reps,* is available from IWS, Inc., for $10. These reps fill out all papers for you and pay fast!

Overseas *import* agents will often handle your *exports!* Thus, an import-export agent in England will be glad to handle *your* exports for a small fee. Since he's dealing with the documents every day of the year, he can fill them out for you faster. Also, he can help speed up the payment to you by the overseas buyer. A number of these import agents are also listed in the above book.

## Ship the items ordered by your customers

By working carefully, you can get your supplier to ship his item to *your* customer. This is called *drop-shipment* and will:

- Save your time
- Save you money
- Get items to your customer faster
- Make your life less complicated

Now I want you to understand one fact clearly. That is:

> Not every supplier will drop-ship for you. But you can get more suppliers to drop-ship if you try to sell them on the idea.

So you see—even in mail-order export—you still have to be a salesman! As my friend Henry Kaiser once said: "Everyone in the world is selling something."

Now I'll admit to you that the papers and documents that have to be prepared for overseas shipment of items can be frightening the first time you see them. But you can do the work yourself if you follow a few simple directions. For a complete guide to preparing the needed documents, buy a copy of the book mentioned above—*How to Prepare and Process Export and Import Documents:* A Fully Illustrated Guide, from IWS, Inc., P.O. Box 186, Merrick, N.Y. 11566. The price of this guide is $25. Having a copy of it on hand can easily save you thousands of dollars in time and mistakes.

You can save time and money in your export activities in other ways, including:

(1) Requiring your suppliers to prepare shipping documents, where doing so would not reveal any of your business secrets.
(2) Requiring customers to supply you with filled-in import documents where they are required. This reduces the time you must spend on them.
(3) Using freight and insurance specialists on a free basis to assist you in figuring the costs and best way to handle the items you export.
(4) Using the free services and advice offered by airlines and shipping firms on the best and cheapest way to ship a given export item.

## Collect your money from your customers

Basically, there are three ways to collect payments for overseas sales:

(1) Cash with order
(2) Cash on delivery
(3) Staggered payments

*Cash with order* is the safest way to be paid for overseas sales. But it's also the most difficult arrangement to negotiate, particularly when you're just starting. However, I personally prefer this way of being paid, even though I recognize that it:

- Can cause loss of orders
- Makes you look "hungry"
- Reduces the speed of making business friends
- Can limit the rate of growth of your business

But cash with order is not all bad. Why? Because:

- You get your money *before* you ship
- There's usually enough time for the check to clear
- You don't spend money and time on unnecessary bill collections

*Cash on delivery* seems like a perfect way to handle exports because you deliver your product and collect your money in one swift step. But life doesn't always work that way because:

- Your shipment may be refused for any number of reasons
- You will have to pay warehouse charges until the goods are delivered if your shipment is refused
- Your exports may be damaged in the warehouse, leading to more problems
- Predictions of the actions of overseas buyers are difficult to make— and the best way to reduce or eliminate problems of this type is to make NO predictions at all!

So you see that C.O.D. can be a problem-maker for you, unless you know your customer. Of course, once you get on a cordial basis with your customers, you can select those with whom you'll work via C.O.D. But as a start, work on the basis of cash with the order. Then you'll have few problems with the collection of your money.

*Staggered payments* are the next best thing to cash with order. When you receive staggered payments you are paid in this way:

(1) A portion of the total purchase price—say 25 percent or 33 percent—with the purchase order.
(2) An equal payment at an agreed-upon later date, prior to the final delivery of the items ordered.
(3) A final payment on delivery of the items ordered.

Why is the staggered payment arrangement a good one for you when you're just starting in export-import? Because:

- There's less danger of a refused C.O.D.
- You're paid as the deal progresses.
- Your only investment is for postage.
- You can't be hurt badly.

## Get your bank to work for you

Many big banks have large, expert staffs who'll work for you *free* of any charge when you deal in export-import items of many kinds and have an account in the bank. "Why will these banks work for me free?" you ask. There are many reasons, including:

- Banks want *all* the business they can get
- Foreign exchange business is *profitable*
- Doing business overseas helps banks *expand*
- Export business is a *paper business*—which all banks love
- Doing business with a domestic exporter can *attract* an overseas customer

"Now how can a bank help me in my export business?" you ask next. Domestic banks can help you in many ways, including:

- Processing letters of credit
- Financing your exports (partially or completely) when necessary
- Preparing export-import documents
- Checking out overseas customers
- Providing up-to-date data on foreign markets
- Giving you the best exchange rate
- Corresponding with overseas customers
- Plus many other services

You may not (and need not) believe what I tell you about the help big banks can offer you in exporting. To verify what I say, just call or write the International Department of any of the following randomly selected banks whose local address you'll find in a large-city telephone book where the bank has a branch:

Wells Fargo Bank
Bank of America

First National City Bank
Chase Manhattan Bank
Manufacturers Hanover Trust
Chemical Bank
Bankers Trust

When you call, ask for an Export Officer. As soon as he comes on the line, ask him what services his bank can offer an export firm or agent such as yourself. You'll be both surprised and delighted by what you hear. For instance, at the time of this writing, the Bank of America had some 700 import-export experts on its staff! And all the other banks listed above also have large staffs.

### Know what your bank can do

Having a bank that can work internationally is your first step in getting free help. To make the best use of your bank's facilities, you must know what your bank can do. As an example of what a bank can do for firms in international business, one bank:

- Will transfer money from one country to another in 24 hours
- Offers import-export credits to help you finance your exports
- Helps you prepare the export documents you need to export specific items
- Will act as the opening and paying bank for you
- Can help you collect the money owed you by your overseas customer
- Supplies "clean" letters of credit for you, reducing the amount of supporting paperwork you need
- Many other helpful services

Now not every bank will offer you *all* these services. So don't expect to get every service you need from *every* bank. Yet some banks may offer you *more* services! The only way to find out is to ask the bank of *your* choice.

Note that the banks listed above are certainly *not* the only ones that can give you export-import help. There are hundreds of others around the United States. All you have to do to check your local bank is to make a quick phone call and ask: Do you help with export-import business?

At the time of the writing of this chapter, U.S. banks had some 600 overseas branches all over the world. Within a few years, there will be 1,000 or more branches. Can you think of any better way to be represented locally than by a big-name bank?

And now that I've told you how to work with a good bank that has widespread overseas offices, take the first step and open a business account at the bank of your choice. You'll be repaid over and over by the many free services you receive.

### Get rich doing things the right way

The 11 steps given you in this chapter aren't the only way to export items to overseas buyers. But these steps are, and have been:

- Proven by actual use
- Practical for you
- Profitable to you

I'm sure that as you gain experience in export-import you will vary some of these steps slightly. Great! Write me a letter telling me how you changed a given step and what results you obtained. If you give me permission to do so, I'll pass your hints along to other export-import operators.

The main intent of the lucky 11 steps listed above is to help you do things the *right* way. Once you start doing things the right way, you earn more from your efforts *sooner,* and with *less* work. Could anything be better for you?

### Move into export riches today!

Seventy-five percent of the more than three billion people in the world today haven't yet reached the bicycle-owning stage in life! Yes, the world's people hunger for the raw materials and manufactured products that can give them a better life. And you can help give them this better life by exporting the items they need. Further, as the income and wealth of overseas people increase, the demand for your exports will grow.

And don't worry about competition. With a market of more than three billion people—and predictions of a market of more than seven billion people in the relatively near future—there aren't enough ambitious and capable business people like yourself to fill the needs! So welcome competition. The more overseas people see your exports, the more they'll want.

In the next chapter you'll read a number of actual stories of how Beginning Wealth Builders (BWB's) use the Easy Mail-Order Export Wealth Success Techniques given in the present chapter. Put these techniques to work for yourself and watch your riches grow and grow in just a few months!

## POINTS TO REMEMBER

- There's an enormous market throughout the world for exports.
- Exporting is a simple "paper" business needing little cash investment.
- You can easily start exporting, using just a letterhead, some stamps, and a few books.
- Your bank will gladly become your export "partner," willing to help in many ways.
- For a sure, easy start in exporting, take the 11 steps given in this chapter.

# 5

## How Big Export Fortunes
## Are Made by Beginners

In the previous chapter you learned the 11 basic steps you can take to build your export business. Now you're ready to see how export fortunes are made, and exactly how you can build *your* riches in the export business.

### Is exporting mail order?

No; the export business isn't the same as the direct-mail or mail-order business, even though the usual export business is carried on almost entirely by mail! Now figure that one out!

That's what Carl L. tried to figure out after making an $80,000 profit during his first year in exporting. Here's how Carl built his profits.

For years Carl L. had idly dreamt about working in his own home at a mail-order business. Why? Because Carl hated to travel any further than to the local golf course. Since the mail box was nearer than the golf course, Carl thought that mail order was his dream business. Further, the sale of products by mail order had a basic appeal to Carl.

Because he disliked all forms of travel, Carl ignored export-import, thinking that this business required worldwide travel.

Actually, the only required travel is between your home and the corner mail box.

## Get the data you need

One evening, while visiting a friend's home, Carl chanced on a copy of *Worldwide Riches Opportunities.* Flipping through this book, he was amazed to see the thousands of overseas firms seeking exported products and raw materials. The instructions included in the book were clear and easy to follow. Carl decided to order a copy of the book for his own use. So he sent $25 to IWS Inc., P.O. Box 186, Merrick, N.Y. 11566, for a copy of Volume 1. Later he ordered a copy of Volume 2 for $25.

When his copy of the book arrived, Carl sat down and studied it in greater detail. He soon learned that exporting *isn't* mail order. But you can hardly get anywhere in exporting without using the mails!

## Make exporting a painless business

Carl was interested in electronics. So he decided to see if this interest could be matched with overseas product and equipment needs. To do this, Carl:

(1) Studied the list of export needs in the book he purchased
(2) Listed the needs in the product area that interested him
(3) Counted the needs

To his delight, Carl found more than 200 firms listed in *Worldwide Riches Opportunities* which sought electronic products or equipment. This number of potential customers, Carl reasoned, was an excellent starting base for his business.

## Learn from past experience

Having been in another business several years earlier, Carl decided that the lessons he'd learned in that business would not be wasted. Those lessons were:

• Avoid every possible business problem.
• Make the smallest possible money investment in a business.

- Invest plenty of time, energy, and skill in the business.
- Try to work just with paper, typewriter, envelopes, and stamps.
- Sell to companies instead of individuals wherever possible.
- Collect as much money in advance as you can.
- Try to develop repeat sales instead of one-shot sales, but keep flexible at all times.
- Make profit your major objective because without a profit a business is just a drain on your energy.

Starting with these concepts, Carl soon built a highly success-full, problem-free export business. Here's how he did it.

## Help your customers place orders

Overseas customers usually have specific product needs, such as:

- Manufactured items
- Raw materials
- Semi-finished products
- How-to publications of all kinds
- Entire plants, factories, and other large facilities
- Both advanced- and low-technology items

Carl isolated "multiple needs" in his *Worldwide Riches Opportunities*. These were duplicate needs expressed by two or more overseas firms. It would be easier, Carl thought, to sell items wanted or needed by more than one buyer.

With this as his guiding idea, Carl typed up a list of electronic components and equipment which he found were needed by overseas buyers. Then he checked a number of electronics catalogs, seeking price data on the items on his list. As a check on the catalogs, he called the firms which had published them and obtained data on discounts and deliveries. With this information in hand, Carl typed up his own four-page catalog. To help his customers order his products, he attached a fifth page containing an easy-to-use order coupon.

## Get your data to your customers

With his typed catalog ready, Carl went to a local offset printer and had 100 copies of each page printed at a cost of 2¢ per page, for a total cost of $10. Carl collated the pages himself on the kitchen table and then stapled each catalog.

With his catalog ready, Carl typed 100 air-mail envelopes, using the company names and addresses obtained from *Worldwide Riches Opportunities*. He also typed 100 air-mail return envelopes to help his customers order more easily. His total cost for the envelopes was $10.50.

## Get your message out to buyers

Next, Carl mailed his catalog to his overseas prospects at a total cost of $50 for postage. But instead of sitting back and doing nothing while waiting for orders to roll in, Carl turned to his copy of *Worldwide Riches Opportunities*, Volume 2, to isolate other multiple needs. Within a few days, he had multiple listings of overseas firms needing three other items that he knew he could supply.

## Build your business fast

Carl's work paid off quickly. Within a week of his first mailing, he received his first order for electronic components. And, good news, the order was accompanied by a check for $2,750! This first check more than paid for:

- *Worldwide Riches Opportunities*, Volumes 1 and 2
- Printing of product data
- Overseas mailings
- Printing of return envelopes

Carl's profit on his first order was $268–a little less than 10 percent. This is excellent, when you stop to think that most new businesses lose money during their first year. Carl–by following the Hicks recommendations in this and the previous chapters–made a profit during his first month!

Carl's first order was followed by fourteen other orders during the following ten days. Some orders were larger than the first; some smaller. But Carl's total profit during his first month in business was $3,874! Not bad on an investment of less than $200!

When Carl analyzed his investment in his new business, he found that his biggest outlays were:

- Time (which costs nothing when you're poor)
- Energy (which most people have)
- Paper (costs little)
- Postage (the world's best bargain)

This brings us to an important money-making principle for you:

> The fewer the items (raw materials, machinery, personnel, and so forth) you need for your business, the sooner you can show a profit.

## Grow rich on paper

Thousands of Beginning Wealth Builders consult me in person and as subscribers to the monthly newsletter *International Wealth Success* about going into business for themselves. When they like mail-order type businesses I tell them:

> Build a fortune out of paper. All you need is a letterhead and some stamps and you can become an "Instant Millionaire."

Thousands of people become rich this way every year without:

- Ever seeing the product they sell
- Ever touching the product
- Ever doing hard physical work

Carl built, and runs, a paper empire that delivers more than $100,000 a year in profits to him in his home. You can do the same if you just keep in mind this important principle:

> "Paper" businesses can be just as profitable as any other business, and can be started for a much smaller investment on your part.

But let's say that you want to avoid the fuss and bother of export forms and similar documents. Is there any route you can take to export riches? Yes, there is.

### Export the painless way

Some of my friends hate paperwork of all kinds. They much prefer face-to-face dealings with prospective buyers. Yet these same BWB's want to get into the export business. How can they? Here's how.

Paul P. is a man I describe as a paper-hater. He:

- Abhors paperwork
- Loves on-the-spot selling
- Is an excellent talker
- Dresses well
- Likes the idea of exporting

"Paul," I said during his first talk with me, "you're a capable guy, and I want to see you make it big in exporting without getting involved in a yard of paperwork on each deal!"

"Ty," he said, "now you're talking my language. But how can I get around having to fill out those reams and reams of customs documents?"

"There really aren't reams of documents, Paul," I said. "It just seems that there are!" Then I told Paul how to export "without papers." You can do the same. Here's how.

### Use your head to build export riches

In nearly every country of the world, there are industrial representatives on the embassy staffs sent overseas to represent one country in another country. These reps can act for:

- Their government
- Firms in their country
- Individuals in their country

Now let's say that a large firm overseas seeks the product you export. But you would prefer to avoid all the paperwork. What can you do? Here are five lucky steps you can take to build great wealth by exporting without large amounts of paperwork:

(1) Contact by mail, phone, or in person, the embassy industrial rep of the country to which you plan to export—for example, France.

(2) Tell the rep the name of the firm in his country (France, in this case) to which you plan to export.

(3) Explain to the rep that you would like to have him, or his agency, handle the export of the items sought by the firm in his country. (To arrange such a deal you may have to take the rep to lunch or dinner once or twice because such deals are often put together outside the office.)

(4) Have the rep contact the firm in his country; have him ask if his handling of the export details (*not* the financing) will be acceptable to your customer. (It usually will be.)

(5) Go ahead with the deal after you obtain written or verbal notice from the rep that your customer will let him (or his embassy) handle the export arrangements.

Returning to Paul's case, which we mentioned earlier, we can see how such an arrangement with a rep can work out. Here are the details.

## Sell here for profits there

Paul's a born salesman. He loves to talk to people, to sell them his product. But first Paul had to learn whom he should be talking to in the various embassies. To get the rep's names, Paul obtained a copy of *Addresses of Industrial Reps of Overseas Countries* ($15 from IEA, P.O. Box 525, Hicksville, N.Y. 11802).

With this list in hand, Paul called embassies involved to get the name of the industrial rep. To save money, Paul called after 6 P.M., knowing that most embassies have one or more people on duty until 12 midnight. This worked well at ten of the embassies and Paul spent only $7.20 on calls to get the names of the ten reps. (He could have spent about half this much to obtain the same information by mail but much more time would have been required.) Another reason for calling on the phone is that you get the name of the present rep. With a high turnover rate the reps may change quickly.

Next, Paul arranged sales of items to overseas firms in the ten countries whose rep names he obtained. To make these sales Paul used copies of the monthly newsletter *International Wealth Success* and the publication *Worldwide Riches Opportunities*.

Once the deals were arranged, Paul contacted the industrial reps whose names he had obtained earlier. Most of the reps were delighted to handle the export papers. What was Paul's profit on these transactions? $72,814 in three months! Not bad for a beginner who hates paperwork.

## Mail your way to export riches

Up to now we've been talking about exporting items that fill the specific needs listed in *Worldwide Riches Opportunities.* Another approach to making millions in exporting is to use overseas direct mail. But instead of mailing to overseas consumers, you mail to overseas industrial firms. Why? Because:

- Sales are easier
- You're paid faster
- You have fewer complaints
- Repeat sales are often possible

I call this method *overseas industrial direct mail.*

How do you mail your overseas industrial ads? There are two ways:

(1) Surface mail
(2) Air mail

Use surface mail when: (a) You have the time to wait six weeks for your mail to arrive at its overseas destination; (b) You are trying to save money on postage; (c) You have large, bulky items, such as catalogs, to send to your overseas prospects.

Use air mail for your overseas direct mail ads when: (a) Time is important in the delivery of your ad; (b) You want to impress your overseas prospects with the efficiency of your service; (c) Your mailing material is so light that the extra cost for air mail is not excessive.

Where can you obtain the names of firms for your direct mail ads? Use your copies of *Worldwide Riches Opportunities* and *International Wealth Success.* These handy publications give you the complete firm name, address, products sought, and, in many cases, the name of the individual to whom you should send your direct-mail ads.

## Follow up with easier sales

Once you make an industrial sale using overseas direct mail ads, arrange to have your supplier *drop-ship* the item, if possible. (In drop shipping your supplier ships for you.) This reduces your export paperwork problems. And it is one way to easier sales in overseas industrial mail order.

Another technique for obtaining easier sales is to include a lightweight copy of your catalog with every mailing you make to any overseas contact. This simple method can generate sales for years to come. When thinking of advertising, remember this key fact:

> The cost of printing and mailing a catalog is minute,
> compared with the potential profit you can earn from a
> big overseas sale.

## Build your wealth everywhere

Now before I close this chapter I'd like to tell you about one other Beginning Wealth Builder (BWB), who's hitting it big in exporting and related deals. This BWB—Ray, by name—used a lead in *International Wealth Success* to negotiate a contract to sell 3,000 bushels a month of alfalfa seed to a South American country. All Ray had to do was get a seed seller together with a seed buyer. For arranging the deal, Ray receives a certain monthly commission. The contract is guaranteed by a bank in the seed grower's town.

Shortly after swinging the seed deal, Ray came across an attractive and profitable apartment house costing $87,500 that he wanted to buy. The down payment asked was 20 percent or $17,500. But, like many other BWB's, Ray didn't have the required down payment. Even though he didn't have the money he needed to take over the building, Ray decided to talk it over with his bank.

During the conversation, Ray casually mentioned that he had a contract to supply 3,000 bushels a month of alfalfa seed to a

South American country. The banker's ears immediately perked up. He asked a few questions and then told Ray:

"You can use your seed contract as down payment on this income-producing apartment house and we'll finance the first mortgage—$70,000—for you also!"

Ray was delighted. Why? Because by just investing a few pennies in stamps and paper, he was able to:

- Develop a steady, monthly income from exporting
- Use his export income as collateral for another income producer for himself
- Shelter from income taxes some of his export income with the allowable depreciation on the real estate

Since Ray needed only about 95 percent of his monthly export payment to cover the repayment of the down payment loan, he's receiving 5 percent for himself. Further, he has an excellent monthly income from the rental apartment house taken over by using the bank-guaranteed seed contract! So you see, exporting can make *you* rich.

## You can make it big in exporting

Only about 4 percent of the firms in the United States were exporting at the time of the writing of this book. With such a small number selling items overseas, there is an enormous opportunity for you to strike it rich on a very small start—less than $100. Just use the hints, books, and newsletter listed in this chapter and you'll soon be on your way to the wealth you seek.

### POINTS TO REMEMBER

- Exporting is *not* mail order
- You do *not* have to travel to make it big in exporting
- By taking simple steps, you can make exporting an easy business
- Help your customers place their orders
- Try to isolate customer "repeat needs"
- Sell from catalogs, whenever possible
- Learn how to export the painless way

# 6

# How to Import Worldwide Products
# and Prosper

Importing is the opposite of exporting. When we *import*, we buy products from overseas firms and sell these products in our own country. As an importer, you hope to find a unique product which will have a large sale in your own country.

### Beware of import traps

Many beginners think that importing is the simplest way to riches known to man. "All you have to do is find a good product and then sell it," they say. That's basically true. But take it from Ty Hicks, who has done plenty of importing from throughout the world, that:

- Finding a *good* product isn't always easy
- Controlling product *quality* can be a real problem
- Import *regulations* can be troublesome
- Selling the product in your own country can be the biggest job of all

Now, good friend, don't call me a negative thinker. That I'm not! But I do want to warn you of the day-to-day problems of importing *before* you rush off to buy some foreign products. If you listen to me and follow my advice, you may be able to beat my present record with imports. What's more, it won't cost you anything to listen!

"And what's your record?" you ask. Just this: *Working less than three hours a week on the import business, I've been able to find, and import, products which are currently achieving sales of more than $250,000 per year—$254,336* during the year of this writing. Now if I can do that in less than three hours a week, think of what you can do in 40 hours a week!

### Anybody can make money in importing

"Sure, Ty," you say. "*You* can make sales of a quarter of a million dollars per year in importing. But can *everyone* do the same?" Positively—I reply—if they try. However, you can't just sit back and expect the profits to fall from heaven. But I *can* guarantee you this:

> If you follow my suggestions (altering them to suit local conditions), read, and use the books and other guides I recommend, you can hit the BIG MONEY importing.

To show you that you can easily hit the big money in importing, I'd like to give you a few quick examples of real living people, just like yourself, who hit the big money in importing without:

- Investing large sums of money
- Working long hours
- Selling door-to-door
- Having any special skills or training

Seeing how these "people in the street" made the big time will, I hope, encourage you to do more to build your own success.

### CRIPPLE WORKS AT HOME AND PROSPERS

Sam T. was crippled by an industrial accident and confined to his home. Time hung heavily on his hands because, before his accident, Sam had been a busy and active person. So Sam began to look around for something to do at home that would keep him busy, and possibly increase his income, because his disability payments were small.

Sam was a tropical fish hobbyist. One day, a friend asked Sam if he knew where a rare South American fish could be obtained. Sam didn't know, but he promised to try to find out. This promise led Sam on a two-month mail and phone hunt without turning up one source. "I'd pay anything for such a fish," the friend said when Sam told him of the blanks he'd drawn.

This remark set Sam to thinking. If his friend would pay "anything" (i.e. a high price) for such a fish, would other tropical fish hobbyists do the same? Sam did some quick market research by calling a number of fish hobbyists on the phone. To his surprise, eight out of ten, or 80 percent, said they'd be delighted to pay whatever the going price was, just to be able to get such rare fish. And several suggested other species of fish they'd gladly pay high prices for. The combination of the remark and his research put Sam into the imported fish business.

It didn't take Sam long to take the action needed to convert his market information into money, namely by:

(1) Writing up a list of the fish people wanted
(2) Contacting, by mail, overseas suppliers of tropical fish
(3) Obtaining, by mail, a price list of the fish wanted
(4) Negotiating, by mail, prices on quantity purchases
(5) Working out, by mail, suitable ways to ship purchased live fish by air freight (the fish are sealed in plastic bags of sea or fresh water)
(6) Advertising his service in suitable hobby magazines

Sam's importing business expanded from zero to $5,000 a month in a few months. Fish hobbyists, he found, wanted rare fish of all kinds and were willing to pay high prices to get what they wanted. Since the fish were light and easy to handle, Sam had no shipping problems. Not one fish failed to reach its buyer in a healthy condition.

Today, Sam has a prosperous import business booming for him. Being an invalid, he is delighted that he can conduct his entire business by mail from his home. Sam has *never* had to leave his home to do a single thing for a customer.

## WIDOW MAKES BIG IMPORT PROFITS

When Beverly L's. husband passed on, he left only a few hundred dollars behind him. Beverly was shocked by her loss and frightened by the prospects of supporting herself. But Beverly, like most people, had more courage, creativity, and energy than she either realized or gave herself credit for.

A chance remark by a friend got Bev to thinking. "If I were you, Bev," this friend said, "I'd take this chance to go into business for myself, instead of looking for a job with some big firm." But like most of us, Bev couldn't take action on her dreams immediately. So Bev took a job in a greeting-card store to earn a few dollars to tide her over. Taking this job was the best decision Bev ever made because it put her into the importing business.

At the store, Bev soon noticed that big, expensive greeting and condolence cards of all types were "in." Since there's an enormous profit on a single sheet of paper printed on two sides and folded only twice, and sold at $5 or more, Bev decided to investigate such cards further.

What Bev quickly learned was that fancy, expensive greeting cards:

- Could be printed cheaply overseas
- Were easy to import by air freight
- Are fast becoming status symbols
- Move quickly in the right stores
- Sell faster when printed in four colors

With these facts in hand, Bev checked out several European printers having offices in the United States. Within a few days, she was given cost estimates by the printers for various numbers of cards.

Using her card-shop experience, Bev made some sales estimates of the number of cards that could be sold by the store in which she worked. She also made some estimates of the number of cards she could sell by mail order to greeting-card stores throughout the U.S.

Using these estimates as a guide, Bev placed her first card order using $300 she had borrowed from a friend. Within a few weeks after receiving the cards Bev sold them out for a total of $2,750, more than nine times the cost.

Today, Bev's imported greeting cards are selling at a rate of more than $3-million per year. Besides importing and selling these cards, Bev has:

- Opened her own greeting-card store
- Plans to franchise 36 other card stores
- Gone into manufacturing her own "imports" using printing plates from overseas
- Expanded her imports to include books, paintings, chinaware, and other items

Truly, Bev is living a wonderful life off well-chosen imported products. This life includes:

(1) A high income—more than $100,000 a year—from her business
(2) Worldwide travel at no expense to herself
(3) Mini vacations wherever and whenever she wants them
(4) A safe, secure future with a big pension when she wants to retire

## Make your life a big success

You can have the same sort of profitable income in importing as Sam and Bev. All you have to do is seek out the right import, find a market for it, and then sell, sell, sell! This chapter shows you exactly how to take these important steps. Taking these steps will, hopefully, put you in the big-money chips the same way that the following BWB's were put on wealth-studded roads to wealth:

- Electronic hi-fi equipment built a $4-million fortune in four years for a radio ham who started his import business on $100 borrowed from his brother.
- Housewife is earning a $27,000 a year profit importing wax flowers for re-sale to florists. Her starting capital was just a few postage stamps.
- Farmer is earning $180,000 a year importing exotic foods for restaurants and taverns. He obtained his start-up capital by putting part of his land up for a crop subsidy of $95,000 in one year.
- Real-estate man is earning $110,000 a year importing copper bracelets and necklaces. He got some of his financing and product-source leads from the monthly newsletter *International Wealth Success.*
- Auto mechanic is earning $18,000 a year in his spare time importing foreign auto parts. His starting capital was $56 he saved from his regular pay.
- Accountant is earning $57,000 a year in his spare time selling personal-product imports by mail order. His starting capital was $750, which he borrowed.

Yes, you *can* build fast import wealth in a variety of fields. Now let's see what other features and techniques will be helpful to you in your search for import wealth enthusiasm and results.

But before we move to these features and techniques, let me say one more thing about my own importing activities which will encourage you. When I started my importing activities, I knew nothing about imports, such as:

- Where to find overseas products
- How to process import documents
- When to order products
- What to do about shipping strikes
- Why importing could be enormously profitable

You're about to obtain all these, and many more, facts in this chapter. So you should easily exceed my record in just a few months. Let's get *you* started on doing that right now!

## Why importing can be so profitable

Any business has two basic types of costs in its operation—fixed and variable. A fixed cost is a cost that goes on and on, for one year or longer, whether you sell a penny's worth of product or not. Typical fixed costs are:

- Rent for office, factory, or other quarters
- Insurance for firm
- Management salaries
- Part of the firm's electric and telephone bills

Fixed costs are also called *overhead* costs.

The other type of cost, the *variable cost,* is sometimes also called an *out-of-pocket,* or *oop* cost. Typical oop costs are:

- Materials
- Freight
- Production labor
- Packing
- Postage

The main feature of a variable cost is that you pay it only when you make a product which you plan to sell.

"Now why are we looking at these costs?" you ask. Because they contain the key to why importing can be so profitable. This key is:

> The lower the fixed costs (or overhead) in any business,
> the higher (in general) the profit the business can earn.

In importing, if you can operate from your own home, as many people do, your fixed costs are essentially zero. Hence, all your costs are variable, *you don't spend until you're ready to sell!* So your profit on each sale can be enormous because you don't have any

- Factory
- Large machines
- Big production payroll
- Interest payments on mortgages

## Know the numbers in import profits

"What kind of profit are you talking about?" you ask. I'm talking about a profit of up to 65¢ on $1.00, or 65 percent before taxes. Compare that with the usual profit of 10¢ on $1.00, or 10 percent before taxes, which the typical manufacturing firm earns. Now you see what I mean about the high profits you can earn in importing. These high profits mean:

- You'll get a bigger return for your time
- You can start with an investment of less than $100
- Your wealth will grow faster than in almost any other business

And if you should make a mistake, which I certainly hope you will not, the money you could lose is small. This is particularly true when you compare the potential losses in importing with the potential losses in almost any other business, such as manufacturing.

So you see, importing can be highly profitable, provided you know what you're doing. And the key to knowing what you're doing is your next step towards great wealth.

## Have a market before you buy

Importing is comprised of three basic steps:

(1) Finding your product
(2) Getting your product
(3) Selling your product

The first two steps are relatively easy. You don't have to look too far to find your product. And you'll soon learn how to get it into your home warehouse. What separates the men from the boys is:

## SELLING YOUR PRODUCT

You can import the most beautiful items in the world. But if you can't sell them, you've wasted your time and your money. So that's why I say:

> Have a market for every import BEFORE you buy it.
> Never order an import until you know how many units
> you can sell, and at what price.

To find out how many units of a given product you can sell, you'll have to do some market research. Though this may frighten some people, market research is really easy to do, particularly if you are planning to sell a small number of higher priced items—such as 1,000 units at $25 each. But if you're planning to try to sell one million items at $1 each, your market survey and research work can be a big job. To take the scare out of market research, just think of it as finding out how many people might buy a certain item!

### Quick market survey techniques

For higher priced items you plan to import, you can make a quick market survey by:

(1) Determining how many units other firms are selling. Look at the *Statistical Abstract of the United States*, available from the U.S. Government Printing Office, Washington, D.C. 20402, for a full rundown on unit and dollar sales of various products
(2) Studying the sales of *similar* items in the above reference when data on the exact product are not available
(3) Asking friends and associates if they would buy a given product and what price they'd be willing to pay for it

For lower priced-mass-distribution items such as the Hula Hoop, Yo-Yo, windproof cigarette lighter, and the like, you may not find as much help in the statistical data available to you. Instead, you'll have to develop a market "feel" based on:

(1) Observing what's popular and selling today
(2) Trying to predict what will be popular tomorrow
(3) Watching to see if your predictions come true

Recognize right here and now that:

> The low-priced mass-circulation fad-type item is more subject to public whim than the higher-priced more-useful item. Hence, you'll usually have more trouble making market estimates for fad-type items.

## Pick the "ideal" import

The ideal import for you will usually be:

(1) Strong—not fragile
(2) Light—not heavy
(3) Safe—not dangerous
(4) Cheap—not costly
(5) Shippable by air freight
(6) Quickly available
(7) Unique—not easily duplicated
(8) Solely available to you
(9) Smaller than competing items
(10) Simpler to use than other products

Now *no* import you will find will ever possess *all* these desirable features. But you must be able to compare prospective imports, one with the other, to see which is the most desirable. Also you must be able to judge the probable troubles any import might give you.

Since it's difficult for anyone—and particularly me—to remember all the above factors, I've devised an import rating and profile table for *any* import. This rating and profile table allows you to score—on a numbers basis—any import that interests you.

### Score your imports

Unless you can score an import on the basis of the above, or some similar, factors, your information about it is meagre and uncertain. To score your import, copy the import profile table shown in Figure 6-1 on a sheet of paper.

**Product Import Profile**

| IMPORT CHARACTERISTICS | CHARACTERISTIC SCORE |
|---|---|
| 1. Strength or durability | 0 1 2 3 4 5 6 7 8 9 10 |
| 2. Weight | 0 1 2 3 4 5 6 7 8 9 10 |
| 3. Safety | 0 1 2 3 4 5 6 7 8 9 10 |
| 4. Cost | 0 1 2 3 4 .5 6 7 8 9 10 |
| 5. Shipping method | 0 1 2 3 4 5 6 7 8 9 10 |
| 6. Availability schedule | 0 1 2 3 4 5 6 7 8 9 10 |
| 7. Uniqueness | 0 1 2 3 4 5 6 7 8 9 10 |
| 8. Exclusiveness | 0 1 2 3 4 5 6 7 8 9 10 |
| 9. Overall size | 0 1 2 3 4 5 6 7 8 9 10 |
| 10. Simplicity of use | 0 1 2 3 4 5 6 7 8 9 10 |

Total Score

**Figure 6-1**

### USING THE IMPORT PROFILE TABLE

Let's say you're thinking of importing cuckoo clocks from West Germany. You know the type of clock I mean—it's small, has weights suspended by thin brass chains, and a miniature white cuckoo who comes out of his house every half hour to sing his little song. As soon as you get all the facts on the clock, you sit down to analyze its import profile. Here's the first way you can do this. Later I'll give you another way.

You'll notice that each characteristic listed in Figure 6-1 is scored between 0 and 10. Thus, if the weight of an import were ideal from a shipping and mailing standpoint, you'd score the weight as 10, or perfect. But if the weight was "terrible" from a shipping standpoint (that is, the product was excessively heavy), you'd score it 0. In between you have a range of 1 through 9 to indicate other score values, depending on your analysis of each characteristic.

So, to use Figure 6-1, evaluate each characteristic of your prospective import and on a sheet of paper, copy the number indicating your score for this characteristic. When you're finished, add the individual scores (that is, the numbers you circled) to obtain the total score for the import. My own import experience indicates that prospective import items which score less than a total of 60 points on Figure 6-1 are questionable buys for most importers.

### Get to work on actual samples

Sitting down with an actual sample of the cuckoo clock in front of you, you score this prospective import thus:

| CHARACTERISTIC | YOUR SCORE |
|---|---|
| 1. *Strength, durability.* You think these are only fair for this product so you score them 5. | 5 |
| 2. *Weight.* The product is light—8 oz., or 0.23 kilo—so you rate the weight as highly desirable, or 9. | 9 |
| 3. Safety is superb because this clock won't explode, burn, or poison someone, so you rate it 10. | 10 |
| 4. Cost is fair—that is the exporter is offering you the clock at $3.00 F.O.B. Bremerhaven. You want to sell the clock at $9.95 here, so you rate cost 5. | 5 |

5. Since the clock weighs so little you
   can have it shipped by air—the
   fastest way, and often the cheap-
   est. You rate shipping as 10.                          10
6. Availability is good—your exporter
   says an order can be shipped in one
   week; your rating is 8.                                 8
7. Uniqueness is fair—there are similar
   clocks around; your rating is 6.                        6
8. Exclusiveness is a problem because
   the exporter won't give you exclusive rights unless you sell 1,000
   or more units a year. So your
   rating is 4.                                            4
9. Overall size is good. The entire
   product can be held in one hand.
   Your rating is 8.                                       8
10. The product is fairly simple to use
    so you rate it 8.                                      8

Total score = 73

Since your import profile total score is more than 60, this
product is a good candidate for your import business. Based on
my experience, and the experience of many other businessmen in
importing, I'd say that this could be a profitable import for you.
I'd rather see you paying only $2.25 or $2.50 for it, but in time
you may be able to raise the price to $10.95. However, there are
many reasons—all favorable—for holding the price of this clock—
which is really a novelty—under $10.

## Develop your import product judgment

"But how can I use the import profile when I don't know
anything about the business?" you ask, in a worried tone. You *can*
use the import profile by just using your good, common-sense
judgment. It's really very easy.

To score a particular characteristic of any prospective import,
just pick that number, between 0 and 10, which best represents—
*in your opinion*—the rating you would give this characteristic. Give
a perfect rating a score of 10; a bad rating 0. Do this for all ten
characteristics and then add up the ratings to find your total score.

This import profile has many uses, and it can put money in

your pocket. But one beautiful aspect of it is that the profile is self-correcting. By that I mean that a slight error in judging one characteristic will usually be made up by a slightly higher score for another characteristic. So you really can't go too far off when you use the import profile in Figure 6-1.


## "See" your import's rating

The second way to use Figure 6-1 involves drawing straight lines connecting each of your scores in Figure 6-1. This gives you a graphic profile for your import, as Figure 6-2 shows for a cuckoo clock we looked at above. A few general rules about the profile you get for your import are:

- The more to the left the profile is, the lower the score
- The more to the right the profile is, the higher the score
- The more nearly the profile approaches a straight line on the righthand side of Figure 6-2, the greater the prospects for the import in your market
- Using Figure 6-2 as a guide, on a separate sheet of paper you can easily draw the profiles for a number of imports you are thinking of buying. And if you work with a group of similar products, say clocks, you can quickly develop an "ideal" profile for an import that earns you a big profit. You can then compare new imports with this "ideal" to see how the new import looks from a market standpoint.

| IMPORT CHARACTERISTIC | CHARACTERISTIC SCORE |
|---|---|
| 1. Strength, durability | 0 1 2 3 4 ⑤ 6 7 8 9 10 |
| 2. Weight | 0 1 2 3 4 5 6 7 8 ⑨ 10 |
| 3. Safety | 0 1 2 3 4 5 6 7 8 9 ⑩ |
| 4. Cost | 0 1 2 3 4 ⑤ 6 7 8 9 10 |
| 5. Shipping method | 0 1 2 3 4 5 6 7 8 9 ⑩ |
| 6. Availability schedule | 0 1 2 3 4 5 6 7 ⑧ 9 10 |
| 7. Uniqueness | 0 1 2 3 4 5 ⑥ 7 8 9 10 |
| 8. Exclusiveness | 0 1 2 3 ④ 5 6 7 8 9 10 |
| 9. Overall size | 0 1 2 3 4 5 6 7 ⑧ 9 10 |
| 10. Simplicity of use | 0 1 2 3 4 5 6 7 ⑧ 9 10 |

Total Score:   73

**Figure 6-2**

When you use either form of the import profile, keep this fact in mind.

> An import profile helps you make a business decision. If you don't like what a profile tells you, you can easily over-rule it.

But if you do over-rule an import profile, do it carefully!

### Develop your own system

Now you might not like the scoring system or characteristics which I use in Figure 6-1. If so, don't worry! I won't be offended if you develop a better method. Go right ahead and do so. Just be sure to send me a copy so I can use it in a later book to benefit other readers!

### Where to find profitable imports

To make importing as profitable as possible for the time you invest, you:

- Should pick products quickly
- Make fast market surveys
- Develop import profiles rapidly
- Test the market speedily
- Move into full-scale sales fast

You can find profitable imports faster if you know something about the publications which can help you.

### Know the literature of importing

As I mentioned earlier I'm trying to include in this book as many useful reference pamphlets and brochures as possible. Here are some on various aspects of importing which you might want to read:

## FROM THE SMALL BUSINESS ADMINISTRATION

### Free marketers' aids

Checklist for Successful Retail Advertising, #96
A Pricing Checklist for Managers, #105
Building Strong Relations with Your Bank, #107
Quality and Taste as Sales Appeals, #113
Measuring the Results of Advertising, #121

### Free management aids

Loan Sources in the Federal Government, #52
Reducing Risks in Product Development, #82
Analyzing Your Cost of Marketing, #85
Innovation: How Much Is Enough? #173
Should You Make or Buy Components? #189

### Free department of commerce items*

Index to Foreign Production and Commercial Reports
Office of Minority Business Enterprise; monthly

To find suitable imports quickly, I suggest that you read the monthly newsletter *International Wealth Success* every month. This useful publication regularly lists imports available, as well as:

- Sources of 100 percent financing for businesses
- Real estate opportunities
- Numerous capital sources
- Mail-order lenders
- Compensating-balance loan sources
- Finder's fee opportunities
- Financial-broker deals
- Consulting opportunities

---

*Available from U.S. Department of Commerce, Washington, D.C. 20230.

To receive regularly your issue of this helpful newsletter which has helped make fortunes for a number of its readers, send $24 for a 1-year subscription to IWS Inc., P.O. Box 186, Merrick, N.Y. 11566. You'll be glad you did.

Other useful sources of information about available imports include:

- *Wall Street Journal*
- *Journal of Commerce*
- *Worldwide Riches Opportunities,* Vol. 1 and 2, available at $25 each from IWS at the previously listed address

Although publications are great sources of import leads, you shouldn't overlook actual on-the-spot travel. It isn't necessary for you to visit foreign countries to find imports. But a trip overseas can:

- Bring you closer to your exporters
- Help you understand import export problems
- Give you many product ideas
- Widen your business horizons

So consider taking a trip overseas to explore foreign import sources. You might even want to take one of the low-cost IWS group import-export tours. These tours, which I may on occasion join as a speaker and business adviser, are fun and profitable for everyone. Participation in these tours is limited to IWS subscribers.

### Decide how to sell your import

There are a number of ways you can sell an import. They include:

- Mail order and direct mail
- Sales to retailers
- Catalog houses
- Wholesale

#### MAIL-ORDER SALES

Probably the most profitable way to sell your imports is by mail order. Why? Because you can get a higher price for a specialty item offered direct to your customers through the mail.

But to sell any item by mail order you must know what you're doing. Earlier chapters in this book gave you many hints on mail sales. But if you're new to both importing and mail order, I suggest that you get yourself some specialized training in both fields. So check the local schools in your area for suitable courses. You'll find the *"Starting Millionaire Program"* and *Mail-Order Riches Program*, both available at $99.50 each from IWS Inc., P.O. Box 186, Merrick, N.Y. 11566, excellent self-study courses for giving you the data you need to get started in importing and mail order.

## RETAIL SALES

You can sell imports to *retailers*—that is, large and small stores of all kinds—best by local calls in person. While you might dislike personal selling of this kind, you may be able to sell more units than by direct mail or mail order. So with a big payday in view, you can get out and sell hard!

You can also sell to *retailers* by direct mail and mail order, but:

- Sales take longer
- Number of units ordered may be smaller
- You are uncertain of the results
- Reorders take longer

So I recommend that you use direct mail and mail order for selling to retailers only as a secondary way of moving your imports—unless you decide that you want to make sales to retailers your main source of income.

## CATALOG HOUSE SALES

*Catalog houses* are familiar to most of us. The catalog house prepares a neatly printed annual or holiday catalog, or both, for distribution to prospective direct-mail and mail-order buyers. Today, most of these catalogs are printed in four colors and handsomely illustrated.

To make a hit with catalog houses, do what I've done in my import business. That is, build your fortune quickly by being sure to:

Offer every catalog house as large a discount as you can, and larger than his other suppliers offer him.

This means that you'll probably have to start offering a discount of at least 45 percent—that is $4.50 off on an item having a list or selling price of $10. This means that the catalog house will pay you $10.00 - $4.50 = $5.50 for the item. From this $5.50 you must pay your:

- Cost of the item
- Freight cost in
- Advertising cost
- Packaging cost
- Other costs

Lastly, of course, you must have something left over for profit. Earning a profit on our labor is the name of this game of importing!

To be able to offer the biggest discount to catalog houses:

- Buy items as cheaply as possible
- Price items as high as possible
- Seek large orders from every catalog house
- Limit the number of free samples you give away
- Keep all your operating costs as low as possible

You can make big money selling imports to catalog houses. But you have to use your head, as I've shown you above.

### SALES TO WHOLESALERS

*Wholesale sales* of imports can relieve you of many headaches— if you can find a few real "gunslinger" wholesalers. And what's a gunslinger wholesaler? He's an all-out, gung-ho salesman who really moves imports. He sells your imports to stores, catalog houses, mail-order firms, and others seeking imports.

Typical wholesalers I know operate from cheap office buildings. Their "furniture" is made of cast-off fruit and vegetable crates, or even cardboard boxes. Yet they make huge profits on imports because their:

- Expenses are low
- Turnover is large
- Items move in and out fast

## Keep your overhead low

For instance, one import wholesaler I know on the West Coast pays only $80 a month rent for a second-floor loft space near the waterfront. Yet, during the year of the writing of this book he sold $1,700,000 worth of imports to retailers (stores, mail-order houses, and others). His profit on these sales was more than 12 percent, meaning that he took some $204,000 home to his wife during the year. It is this BWB who told me: "Success is earning more than your wife can spend!"

"While I keep my expenses low, as you recommend, Ty," he says, "I'm still not a success because she can spend every penny I make! But she's fast reaching the point where there's little left she doesn't have. Then I'll be a success!"

To summarize, the best way to sell your import is to:

> Select the major method of sale (such as retail, mail order, and the like) for your import, then promote it in other markets also.

You can make a big, quick fortune in importing if you take my advice at the start and then:

- Improve your methods
- Keep searching for larger sales
- Think success at all times

## Improve your methods

The only constant in life is change. Recognize this fact and resolve that the changes in your life will be for the better, that is, the changes will be:

- Improvements
- Positive—not negative
- Helpful to people
- Good for yourself
- Beneficial to business

To run your import business more profitably, you should have a copy of *How to Prepare and Process Export-Import Documents*, A

Fully Illustrated Guide. This big, 8 1/2 x 11 inch book, designed to lie flat when open, gives you more than 300 pages of the forms and documents you need to be a successful importer or exporter. Available at $25 from IWS Inc., P.O. Box 186, Merrick, N.Y. 11566, it will soon become your day-to-day operating bible. It will also be your guide after you solve two common import problems: (1) when to order your products, and (2) what to do during costly strikes. Let's take a look at each of these problems right now because you're almost certain to meet them in your import work.

### Know when to order your imports

If you're importing Christmas decorations, you don't place your order in November for this year's holiday! "That's obvious," you say. Perhaps it is to you. But too many novice importers have done just that and been stuck with unsalable items for a year or more. The time to order Christmas items is in the *previous* May.

As a general guide, consider using the Hicks Rule for Imports (HRI):

> Order seven months in advance for repetitive holidays,
> five months in advance for repetitive seasons.

You may, as you advance your own business, want to change these rules. Fine! I never "writ" a golden word yet. But the rules will serve as a starting point in developing your import planning. And when doing your import planning, just remember the other Hicks rule:

> In business it always takes you longer and costs you
> more than you figure it will!

With that time-cost rule in mind, let's take a look at a major source of import delays—strikes of various kinds.

### Be ready for costly strikes

If we were to meet to discuss your financial future, you'd probably hear me remark, within the first hour, that "you have to 'beat the system'—*but you must use honest methods at all times.*"

Now such a remark doesn't mark me as an anti-establishment type—instead it marks me as a man who wants to live within the establishment but at the same time accomplish much more than the average person does. You, I believe, must do the same—if you want to accumulate a large sum of money quickly and honestly.

To "beat the system" I mean that you:

- Work while others doze (such as on trains, planes, buses, or in your car)
- Act while others delay
- Overcome while others succumb

It's in the area of strikes that I suggest you spend a lot of time learning how to overcome while others succumb. Here are a few helpful hints I've used profitably.

### Don't let strikes ruin you

I'm not against union labor—as a seagoing Merchant Marine engineer I was a member of several unions. But in the import business there are so many strikes that can ruin you that you must be ready to overcome them. The strikes I'm talking about include:

- Truckers' strikes
- Seamen's strikes
- Longshoremen's strikes
- Tugboat strikes
- Harbor pilot strikes
- Shipyard strikes
- Airline pilot strikes
- Air traffic controller strikes
- Stewardess strikes
- Airport ground personnel strikes
- "Etc." strikes

Now keep in mind that such strikes can occur on both sides of the waters. So strikes can really hurt you in your wallet. And, if you're like me, that's a very sensitive spot!

To prevent strikes from cutting your import profits, take these steps:

(1) Using the list just given as a guide, prepare your own list of the strikes that *might* hit *you*.

(2) Figure out alternate shippers and ways of getting your import (the usual problem in a strike).

(3) List the alternate shippers and ways you found in Step (2).

(4) Contact your alternate shippers—such as small trucking firms, airlines, shipping lines, and so forth. Find out what their fees are, their schedules, and other capabilities.

(5) Try to arrange, with each shipper, a *strike plan*—that is the service they would give *you* if a strike occurred.

(6) Make complete notes, for each shipper, of the names, titles, phone numbers, work schedules, and other relevant data, of important people at the alternate shipper, as you talk. Then you'll be ready to take action, if and when a strike occurs.

(7) Keep alert to labor news in those industries which affect your business. Then you'll be ready for a strike *before* it occurs.

(8) Take particularly strong pre-strike action if non-delivery of your import items means a loss of steady customers. Do the same if you're in a seasonal business and a strike means the loss of your products for the season.

You *can* beat strikes in the import business. But you must be prepared. Take the steps listed and there will be few strikes that will beat you.

## Keep alert to popular fads

You can make a quick bundle of money in importing from a popular fad such as the Hula Hoop, Yo-Yo, American-flag decals for windows, or other novelties. But you must be alert so you can "tune in" on the fad while:

- It is still new
- You have time to design *your* product
- You contact your overseas suppliers
- The products are shipped to you

- You begin your sales campaign
- You get rich from the deal

By keeping alert to new trends you will be able to move with speed, when you have to. And in today's fast-moving world, speed often means the difference between high profits and no profits.

## Look ahead to your import wealth

You *can* get rich in importing if you really try. I'm just a skinny little guy—5'-10", 134 pounds. Yet with little more than one finger and a few minutes a week, I'm supervising the selection and sale of imports generating more than $250,000 per year in sales! Meanwhile, I'm the busy president of a $2-million-per-year capital lending and personal finance organization "crying" to make loans to people needing money, a big-business corporation executive, president of a moderate-size and highly successful mail-order and direct-mail corporation, owner of several lucrative businesses (lecturing, consulting, and manufacturing), and author of some 33 published books. Now I'm not telling you this to please my ego. Instead, I'm saying:

> If one slender person can do all this, just imagine how
> successful you can be if you just concentrate on
> importing!

So you see, you *can* be a big success in importing. Just recognize that you'll be most successful if you keep the following in mind:

### POINTS TO REMEMBER

- Be aware of import traps
- Recognize the profitability of importing
- Have a market *before* you import
- Make sensible market surveys
- Pick the "ideal" import
- Develop your import product
- Decide how to sell your import
- Improve your methods as you gain experience

- Keep alert to popular fads
- Look ahead to your import wealth

This chapter showed you exactly how to take each of these steps. Now all you need do is get up and walk toward your import riches!

# 7

# Find, Consult, or
# Broker—for Big Fees

When Beginning Wealth Builders (BWB's) ask me "Where should I start my wealth search?" I often say: "Start in a 'paper' business." And what, you ask, is a "paper" business?

### Get to know "paper" businesses

The way I define a paper business—and I think that this may be the first time you've seen such a definition in print—is:

> A paper business is one in which you do not need to own land, machinery, or other expensive equipment to make a profit. Instead, most of your business is done with pieces of paper—such as letters, orders, bills, checks, contracts, and so on.

The profits in a "paper" business can be just as high as in any other business. But the headaches can be far fewer and much less intense. Of course, if you want to grow as big as General Motors, you'll eventually need a factory, land, machinery, and other equipment and facilities. But right now I don't think you aspire to the size of GM because its annual output is greater than that of many of the world's small countries!

125

### Pick your paper business

Any paper business is easy to pick once you decide what you want to do in life. And choosing what you want to do is easier if you understand:

- What a paper business is
- Which paper businesses are profitable
- How you can start *your* business
- When to push for higher profits
- Why you can build enormous income

Let's take a look at each of these items so we can put you into the *big* money sooner.

You read the definition of a paper business at the start of this chapter. Hence, I don't think we need say anything more now. Further, the definition will become clearer as we go along in this chapter.

### Know which paper businesses pay big

Today there are many paper businesses you might choose. But in my opinion—based on hard, practical, and actual money-making experience—the best paper businesses are:

- Finding for fees
- Consulting for fees
- Brokering for fees
- Mail order
- Export-import
- Franchising

We'll look at the first three businesses in this chapter. The other three businesses are discussed in other chapters in this book.

But before we start, take my word for it that you can readily make a million dollars, or more, in any of these paper businesses. All you need do is set your mind to it and work hard!

### Find for enormous fees

The easiest profession to enter in the world today is that of a *finder*. "And just what is a finder?" you ask.

> A finder is a person or firm who, or which, locates, finds, or otherwise obtains something desired by someone else; the finder is paid an agreed-on fee for performing this service.

And what do finders find? Thousands of items, hundreds of people, and plenty of money. Typical items that finders locate include:

- Business real estate properties
- Scarce materials, metals, minerals
- Buyers of specified items
- Money for business purposes
- Companies for acquisition
- Personnel for important jobs
- Plus many, many unusual items

## Questions and answers on finders' fees

To help you understand the finder profession better, here are the answers to your most-likely-to-be-asked questions.

*Q.* What are the usual finder fees which I would be paid as a finder?

*A.* Finder fees vary from a low of 0.5 percent on very large deals to a high of 10 percent on small deals. But you will hear of higher fees for unusual or especially difficult finder tasks. For instance, the finder's fee for locating and hiring a top executive often equals his annual salary. For a $100,000-per-year company president, your fee would be a pleasant year's earnings! (And you could be finding other items during the time you're looking for him.)

*Q.* How are finder fees figured?

*A.* Finders' fees are usually based on the value of the item found. Thus, you'll find that the fees are usually stated as follows:

| ITEM | FEE BASIS |
|---|---|
| Real estate | Percent of property cost |
| Loans; financing | Percent of money borrowed |
| Materials; minerals; machinery | Percent of item cost |
| Personnel | Percent of annual salary |

The cost in three of the above cases (first, third, and fourth) is what your client (who is usually the buyer, but may also be the seller) pays for the item you find for him. Thus, if you find minerals such as sulfur for which your client pays $100,000 and your finder's fee is 8 percent, your dollar fee is 0.08 ($100,000) = $8,000.

*Q.* Where can I set up my finder's business?

*A.* Anywhere in the world! Almost all finder deals are negotiated by mail. So if you're served by the post office, you can be a finder.

*Q.* What's the best way for me to get started as a finder?

*A.* You can have your letterheads printed, register your business (if necessary in your state), and then look for business by advertising in local papers, in national trade magazines, industrial directories, and similar publications. If you start this way you'll just stumble along, learning by hit and miss. But if you want to start quickly and easily, making the fewest mistakes possible, I suggest that you see the IWS *Financial Broker-Finder-Business Broker-Consultant Program.* This big *Program* has *exact* instructions on how to:

- Set up your business
- Get free publicity
- Find clients
- Negotiate fees
- Protect your fees

To obtain this *Program* with its four personalized diploma-like colorful certificates giving you membership in the IWS Finder's Association, Financial-Broker Association, Business-Broker Association, and Business-Consultant Association, send $99.50 today to IWS Inc., P.O. Box 186, Merrick, N.Y. 11566.

*Q.* How much can I earn as a finder?

*A.* There's really no limit—some finders receive fees as high as one million dollars for one deal! But from a practical standpoint, you can expect your first finder fees to be a few hundred or a few thousand dollars. Thus, one user of the IWS *Program* mentioned above earned $2,150 as his first finder fee. This paid the cost of his *Program* by more than 21 times!

*Q.* Would it be possible to be cheated out of a finder's fee?

*A.* Yes—it might be possible to be cheated out of a finder's fee. But this never happens if you carefully arrange your business deals.

*Q.* Can I run a finder business from my home?

*A.* You sure can! And, if you want, you can run your finder business by mail, from your home. As a finder, you never need tramp around to look for things, unless *you* choose to do so. You can find what you are looking for by glancing over newspapers, magazines, catalogs, and similar sources of information, or by calling people on the telephone.

*Q.* Where can I locate sources of finders' fees?

*A.* One of your best sources of finders' fees is the monthly newsletter *International Wealth Success.* This interesting and profitable newsletter regularly publishes a variety of finder fee offers. To start your finder business from one of these offers all you need do is negotiate the deal, after contacting the individual or firm making the offer. To obtain your monthly copy of this excellent newsletter, send $24 for a one-year (12-month) subscription to IWS Inc., P.O. Box 186, Merrick, N.Y. 11566.

## Become a highly paid consultant

The second paper business which you might like to consider is that of becoming a highly paid business consultant. Some consultants earn as much as $4,000 per day, plus expenses. As a beginner, you should earn at least $250 per day, plus expenses. With more experience, your daily fee (called your *per diem*) should rise to $300, $400, $500, and higher. Any expenses related to your work with the client, such as:

- Travel fare (planes, trains, taxis, and other transportation)
- Entertainment of customers at night clubs, ball games, theater, and other amusements
- Hotel lodging
- Meals
- Telephone, telegraph
- And so forth

are billed by you to your client. This means that you might have, say, $853 in expenses in one day for travel, meals, and entertainment, which your client pays. Besides these expenses, you would also receive your daily fee—completely free and clear. Thus, with a daily fee of $500, your income for the day would be $500 + 853 = $1,353. Out of this you would, of course, pay the expenses of $853, leaving you $500 for yourself.

As a business consultant, you are classed as an *independent contractor* for income-tax purposes. This means that—at the present time—there are *no* withholding or Social Security taxes taken out of your fees. When you earn $500 a day, that's what you receive. (Of course, you *must* pay your income and Social Security taxes on the consulting fees you earn. But you pay these on a quarterly basis.) Now let's answer some questions you might have about becoming, and being, a consultant.

## Questions and answers for would-be consultants

*Q*. What can I consult about?

*A*. Almost any *business* subject you know well. Thus, you might be a consultant on:

- General management
- Accounting, bookkeeping
- Taxes and tax management
- Personnel development
- Industrial maintenance
- Purchasing for business
- Business financing

*Q*. What kinds of firms can I consult for?

*A*. Any firm needing your help is a potential client for you. Such firms can include:

- Manufacturing
- Service
- Mining
- Agricultural
- And so forth

*Q*. What's the best way to make big money fast in business consulting?

*A*. *Get a specialty and follow it.* Don't worry about the

uniqueness of your specialty—the most unusual your special area, the greater your chances of getting good, high-paying consulting assignments. Thus, I know people who consult in these special areas:

- Auto wrecking yards
- Marina operation
- Airport runway construction
- Small business accounting
- Wealth building for beginners

*Q.* Where can I get help on becoming a business consultant?

*A.* There are only three places I know of where you can get help: by (1) talking to consultants in the business, (2) reading an interesting book called *The Business Healers,* by Hal Higdon published by Random House, and (3) the IWS *Financial Broker-Finder-Business Broker-Consultant Program.* This helpful program shows you exactly how to start and succeed in your own consulting business without investing more than a few dollars. To get your copy of this helpful program send $99.50 today to the address mentioned earlier in this chapter. You will also receive four handsome diploma-like certificates with your program.

## Make big money as a financial broker

The nicest paper business—in my opinion—is that of brokering, and, in particular, financial brokering. Why do I say this? Because I've been a financial broker of sorts all my life, bringing money and people together. This fun business has made me a pile of money but—more important—it has also:

- Showed me how many firms work
- Pointed up high-profit businesses
- Made hundreds of good friends
- Kept me close to thousands of money sources

You can do the same if you wish. And I hope you at least consider making your fortune as a financial broker. Why? Because in just learning about this great profession you'll improve your earning ability! Truly, you earn while you learn.

## Earn $5,000 an hour

Before I tell you about how you can earn up to $5,000, or more, an hour, let's get a few special words clearly understood. Then it will be easier for you to move ahead faster.

Your first special word is *broker*. A broker is anyone who works to bring two or more people or organizations together to complete a deal. Thus:

- *Real-estate brokers* bring people together for the buying and selling of property, buildings, homes, factories, and other facilities.
- *Yacht brokers* act in the buying and selling of yachts, boats, and related marine items.
- *Financial brokers* bring lenders and prospective borrowers together to negotiate a loan, the underwriting of stock in a corporation, the purchase of corporate bonds, and other financial transactions. The financial broker is paid a fee, plus his direct expenses, for his services. The usual fee structure begins at 10 percent of the loan negotiated and goes down to 1 percent, or less, for extremely large loans. And on many loans you, as a financial broker, might work out special terms to suit yourself and your client. These special terms might include a "piece of the action"—that is, partial ownership of the business being financed, and a share of the profits of the business. Such terms can really zoom your wealth overnight!
- *Marriage brokers* bring two people together for the purpose of marrying.

As a financial broker you will learn the universal meaning of the famous line: "A beautiful woman is welcome everywhere." This is so true. Business, too, has its "beautiful woman"—the financial broker! Why? Because:

> Every business, small or large, eventually needs borrowed money, venture capital, or some other kind of funds. As a source of these funds, you are welcome eveywhere in the world of business.

"Now, how can *I* earn $5,000 an hour?" you ask. "As a financial broker," I reply. "Give me a for-instance," you say, half-serious, half-jokingly. Fine—here's your real-life "for-instance."

## Make money finding money

Tom L., a real-estate salesman in a midwestern city, was friendly with many local businessmen. As their friend, he often listened to their tales of business woe. Thinking about this one summer evening, Tom suddenly realized an important fact:

> Almost every business problem can be solved by an input of extra money for some purpose, such as: more advertising, new machinery, extra help, or an expanded plant.

"If I could find the money these businesses need," Tom said to himself, "I could really help them while I help myself." With this thought in mind, Tom resolved to try to find the money for the next attractive deal he heard about.

## You can get fast results

Tom didn't have to wait long. Within a week, a local toy manufacturer told Tom about his need for a $200,000 five-year loan. "I'll try to get you the loan if you'll pay me a 5 percent commission," Tom said. "Shake; you have a deal." the manufacturer replied. But just to be sure, Tom jotted down in longhand the agreement below.

June 27, 19——

Dear Mr. ————:

Thanks for agreeing to pay me a 5 percent commission as my Financial Broker fee for finding your firm a $200,000 loan within the next 90 days. We hereby both understand that if I find a lender willing to make this loan within the next 90 days and if your firm accepts a loan in the amount of $200,000 from said lender, I will be paid a fee of $10,000.

If your firm refuses to accept the loan for any reason, then my fee will still be paid by your firm. Further, we both agree that the interest rate on this loan cannot exceed 10 percent per year.

If this letter clearly and accurately states and summarizes our verbal

agreement, kindly sign one copy of this letter and return it to me for
my files.

Very truly yours,

_____

Agreement Accepted


_____

John J. Doe, President, Doe Manufacturing Company


_____

(Date)

## Never stop looking

With his signed agreement in his pocket, Tom asked the
manufacturer to list the assets, or holdings, of the company.
Here's what this list contained:

| ASSETS | ESTIMATED VALUE |
|---|---|
| Land | $ 60,000 |
| Factory building | 30,000 |
| Production machines | 35,000 |
| Office machines | 15,000 |
| Other equipment | 40,000 |
| Total | $180,000 |

Now let's look at where Tom stood. He had:

(1) A signed financial broker agreement
(2) Assets nearly equal in value to the loan needed

With these two items in hand, Tom began to shop for lenders. He:

(1) Called local banks
(2) Contacted large finance firms
(3) Advertised (free of charge, as a subscriber) in the _Inter-
    national Wealth Success_ newsletter
(4) Wrote to many of the lenders listed every month in the IWS
    newsletter
(5) Told local businessmen he was in the market for a $200,000
    business loan

Just 59 days after he made his first contact with the toy maker, Tom found a lender. The loan went through quickly because the assets of the borrowing firm nearly equalled the loan requested. Tom closed the deal in about two hours of actual working time. Since his commission was 5 percent, or $10,000 on the $200,000 loan, Tom figured he made $10,000/2 = $5,000 per hour on the deal!

But what Tom didn't realize was that his first steps toward starting a new career as a financial broker would pay off for years to come. Here's how.

(1) Local businessmen sought Tom out to tell him about their money problems.
(2) He received free invitations to many local business dinners, parties, trips, and social affairs.
(3) Local bankers called Tom and said "Please keep us in mind when you come across a promising business deal. We have plenty of money we want to put to work."
(4) Real estate agents, auto dealers, local tradesmen, and other powerful people called Tom, offering discounts, special deals, and other tokens of friendship.
(5) Tom's *International Wealth Success* ad paid off with more than 100 replies, some of which offered him money to put into local businesses, and others which promised fat fees and other goodies if he could find money for specific firms.

Today, two years later, Tom is riding high in his local area. "I'm a 'wanted' man," Tom says with a happy grin. "People 'throw' money at me in the morning, pleading with me to invest it in a booming young company. In the afternoon, other people beg me to find them money for their young, about-to-boom company. All I have to do is bring the two together to earn my fee. It's the easiest work I've ever done—and positively the most profitable."

## Start brokering today

Being a financial broker might make you happy, rich, and contented. I don't know. But you can get some idea of your

reaction to this profession by sitting down some quiet evening and
imagining yourself:

(1) Looking for loan sources
(2) Negotiating loan deals
(3) Talking almost endlessly with borrowers
(4) Attending parties, meetings, and similar business functions
(5) Handling simple paperwork

The best guide that I know of to becoming a financial broker is
the IWS *Financial Broker-Finder-Business-Broker Consultant Program*, mentioned earlier in the chapter. Costing only $99.50, it
could really put you into a new high-earning career in your own
business. Also, it might improve your social life if you're looking
for new friends and have a desire to be wanted.

## Listen to your good friend

As I've often said in my five other best-selling money books,
listed at the front of this book, the best friend you have in the
world is me—if you want me for a friend. The ideas, advice, and
suggestions I give you are based on a genuine affection for every
Beginning Wealth Builder (BWB) everywhere. Truly, friend, I have
nothing to sell you except *your success!* And, as a man once said,
and as I personally know from seeing thousands of BWB's hit the
big money, "Nothing succeeds like success,"—particularly *your*
success.

So when I suggest that you consider doing things *my* way at the
start, please remember that the suggestions are aimed at:

• Making you richer, faster
• Showing you workable methods
• Saving you wasted time and energy
• Helping you as a friend

Since I've made big money for years (and *still* do) as a
consultant, lecturer, author, publisher, financial executive, real-
estate operator, and financial broker, I believe that I have some
valuable ideas for you which will multiply your chances for
success in any of these fields. I want to make *you* so successful

that you'll come out on my yacht some day and say: "Now, Ty, I'd like to teach *you* a thing or two that you don't know!" Great; I'd love to have you aboard, and would rejoice over everything you taught me! But until that day comes, here are a few examples of traits you, my good friend, might develop in *your* finding, consulting, and brokering personality. In discussing these profit-building traits, I also point out some smart-money operating methods you might consider using.

## Be daring in your paper business

As a finder, consultant, or broker you'll usually work on your own, with no boss telling you what to do. To make big money on your own you must be:

- Daring
- Creative
- Determined

And to show you how each of these traits or characteristics can help you, I'd like to give you a few real-life examples.

### DARING COURAGE PAYS OFF

Barbara M. is a finder with just two years' experience. Yet she's willing to be daring when she thinks it will pay off for her as a finder. Here's how Barbara puts her courage to work in one part of her business.

The usual finder waits for someone to come to him or her with a need that is to be filled. Barbara reverses this procedure, at times. When she finds something she thinks people will later want her to find, she takes an *option* on the item for a very small cash deposit. Then, when she's asked to find *that* item, she can produce it instantly, for a fat fee and profit.

Thus, Barbara, who specializes as a finder of better grade textile materials, textile machinery, complete factories, and similar products, recently bought up, on option, an entire load of unusual tapestry materials for a deposit fee of only $250. Three months later, when she was asked to find (for a fee) the type of tapestry material she had on option Barbara simply lifted her phone and called her supplier. Within hours she had delivered the tapestry material. And in a few days she received her finder's fee—$3,250.

"But how is this being daring," you ask. Barbara is being daring when she puts up her own money to take an option on an item she *thinks* will be in *future* demand. If she doesn't find someone who wants her to *find* her optioned item she'll lose her money when the option runs out in 90, 180, 270, or 360 days. If you don't believe this takes daring, just think about putting up *your* money for something you may never sell.

## MAKE CREATIVITY PAY OFF

Doug M. became a financial broker by using the IWS course you read about earlier in this chapter. He was most grateful for the opportunity offered by this course. Why? Because until the time he took the course, Doug had worked as a mine laborer. Within three months after taking the course, Doug negotiated nearly a million dollars worth of loans!

But besides being ambitious, Doug was also creative. When a new client asked him to negotiate a compensating-balance business loan, Doug found that the local banks weren't too interested. But through his study and reading of good financial books, Doug had heard of a technique which uses city and state bonds to achieve the same effect as a compensating-balance loan. Here's how Doug used his creativity to make money for himself and his client.

You can buy long term city or state tax-free bonds for very large discounts when they *do not* carry an interest coupon. Thus, you could (at the time of this writing) get a $5,000 25-year no-interest bond for $1,200. But if you take this bond to the bank to use it as collateral on a loan, you may be able to get up to $5,000, the face value of the bond!

Using this approach, Doug had his client (a company) buy 30 bonds for a total investment of $36,000. Then Doug took these thirty $5,000 bonds to a local bank which had earlier refused to make him a compensating-balance loan for his client. When he presented the bonds as collateral, Doug received immediate approval by the bank of a $150,000 loan for his client!

Using the innate creativity that I know you have, you can do as well as Doug has. You do, of course, need good introductory training. But once you get your start, I'm sure you'll do well—if you use your brain to be more creative about money matters.

## DETERMINATION CAN UNCOVER MONEY

The world of money is constantly changing. A lender who's your friend today may seem to "hate" you tomorrow. Next week, you may not be able to get rid of him—he'll plead with you to put his money into good, profitable deals.

How can you best deal with these changing attitudes if you're working as a finder, business broker, consultant, or financial broker? One highly successful way of dealing or coping with changing money outlooks is to "bull your way on through," that is, keep trying until you get what you want.

Mel T. did just that when looking for a $100,000 start-up loan for a new business. He contacted 60 lenders before he found one who would say yes to his client's loan application. Just think of that: 59 lenders said no! Yet Mel didn't give up. He was determined to get the loan for his client, and he did!

Note that the three traits or characteristics we've been talking about will work both for your clients, and for yourself, no matter what business you may be in. So start today to develop greater:

- Daring
- Creativity
- Determination

If you take my advice and strengthen these characteristics in yourself you will soon see a big improvement in your money-making ability. So listen to your good friend and consider taking the actions I advise. I have nothing to sell you except your *great* success! So act today, here, *now* for your own future.

And now I'd like to give you 26 wonderful fortune-building ideas. Here they are.

## Twenty-six fortune-building ideas

Always charge for your services—clients value more highly what they must pay for!

Be alert for new business wherever you go—constant alertness pays big returns.

Charge high fees for your services but give new businesses a break by lowering your starting fees.

Develop new skills whenever you can; then sell these skills to your clients.

Evaluate every new client's ability to pay; then charge accordingly—high fees for prosperous clients, lower fees for new businesses.

Follow-up on your clients regularly by mail and phone—this will bring you more business.

Generate new business everywhere. Take on more than you can handle and you'll always have a high income.

Handle all clients politely but firmly—don't be wishy-washy about anything—recommendations, bills, or contracts.

Insist on a written agreement for every job, loan, or deal with *every* client. There will be plenty of times when you'll be glad "it's in writing."

Join a helpful association, such as the International Financial Broker's Association, your local real estate association, or local business group.

Keep written records of all deals, jobs, and business agreements. Never trust your memory, or the other guy's.

Learn something new every day of the year. New knowledge will put new money in your pocket.

Modernize your thinking by reading widely, listening more, and talking less.

Never pay front money—that is, fees to get loans or other deals before the loan or deal is approved.

Organize your work day so you accomplish as much as possible; make every moment pay.

Plan your future growth in your career, your business, and your life. Remember—the future belongs to those who plan.

Question every fact you don't understand. Answers to your questions will often improve your skills and income.

Remember that business has one main objective—to earn a profit. If you can help a man or a firm earn a profit, you have earned your fee.

Study regularly to increase your skills. You have more earning power when you're smarter!

Try to find one new client a week. This will give you about 100 clients in two years, enough to keep you in a new Cadillac, big yacht, and daily caviar!

Use your head—that's what clients pay you to do. Think as much and as often as you can; try to find ways to make money for your clients.

Verify facts—don't take anyone's word on important matters without checking the accuracy of the information.

Watch out for cheats—most clients are honest but some are careless and can cause you to lose money.

"X-ray" every deal for hidden traps. Don't lose money because you failed to check a deal out.

You are the most important person in the world to yourself. Remember this fact and you'll never run down your life-drive by silly self-criticism.

Zero in on problems quickly. Don't waste time "getting ready" to work. Instead, go to work—and make your fortune! *Do it now!*

Yes, good friend, the finding, consulting, and brokering professions can earn you big money. You now know how to get started. All you need do is take that first big step. Good luck!

## POINTS TO REMEMBER

- "Paper businesses" can be highly profitable to you.
- Pick your paper business carefully.
- Consider being a finder—you can earn big fees in this profession.
- Combine finding with financial brokerage, business sales and consulting for a profitable paper business of your own.
- Many finder deals can be negotiated by mail.
- Train yourself using *good* materials and you'll profit enormously.
- Finding, brokering, and consulting can often lead you to business profits of your own.
- As a financial broker you can easily become the most popular person in town!

# 8

# Borrow Your Way to
# Great Wealth

Do you think the words *borrowing, lending, financing, debt, loan,* and *note* are nasty? If you do, friend, I want you to change your opinion of these words—here and now! Why? Because:

> Borrowing and financing for business uses are definitely
> in, throughout the world. You can, if you want to,
> borrow your way to wealth today.

**Move fast toward your wealth**

To build wealth fast you must move with the times. And these times, friend, are the times of the borrowed buck! The true road to wealth these days is by OPM—*other people's money*. And I'm about to give you thousands of OPM leads that tell you:

- Why OPM can make you rich
- What kinds of money are available
- How much OPM *you* can get
- When to apply for your OPM
- Where to get the OPM you need

So let's start—here and now—to make you rich, rich, rich, on other people's money. Read this chapter carefully because I'm about to give you the secret of the century!

## Why OPM can make you rich

In the building of great wealth there are three elements you deal with:

- Ideas
- Money
- Energy

As you know, I talk to thousands of beginning wealth builders (BWB's) every year. And each time I meet a BWB I'm delighted to note that his or her *ideas* for building great wealth are usually good. I seldom meet a BWB who has poor business ideas. Why? Because by the time I meet the usual BWB he has been over his ideas so many times that he has improved them to the point where they are ready for use. So the BWB has one-third of the key to great wealth.

But most BWB's lack the middle third of their wealth formula. This middle third is a five-letter word spelled MONEY. What the average BWB needs is the boldness and imagination to get his business money.

Now most BWB's, besides having good ideas, have a driving energy to get rich soon. So you can say that as a BWB you have the first and third parts of the wealth success equation. You just lack the middle third—*money*—and, perhaps, the boldness and imagination needed to get OPM into your pocket.

As a BWB with good business ideas and enormous drive, all you need do is add money and you can get the greatest wealth-building combination known! And if this money is OPM, you can have the most powerful leverage available to man put to work for you.

OPM can make *you* richer, faster, and easier because with OPM you:

- Work harder
- Feel free, good, happy
- Plan more
- Achieve your goals sooner
- Expand to new income sources
- Keep driving ahead to greater wealth

**What kinds of OPM are ready for you**

You can get two basic kinds of OPM in this world today:

- Debt money
- Equity money

Let's take a quick look at *your* two kinds of OPM so we're clear on the meanings of each kind.

## KNOW THE FACTS ABOUT DEBT MONEY

*Debt money is borrowed money.* You *must* repay debt money either quickly (a *short-term* loan), or less quickly—a *long-term* loan. But either way, you *must* repay the loan. A short-term loan is one you repay in 36 months, or less; a long-term loan is paid off in 37 months, or more.

You can get debt money from these sources:

- Loans—there are hundreds of different kinds
- Bonds—can be sold by your corporation
- Factoring—bill collection in advance

But no matter what the source of your debt money is, you *must* keep one fact in mind at all times:

> Debt money must be repaid—sooner or later. And the need to repay debt money can be a burden on you and your business.

## KNOW THE FACTS ABOUT EQUITY MONEY

*Equity money is cash obtained by selling part of your business.* Equity money is the other kind of OPM you can use in your business. There are two key features about equity money that you may want to keep in mind:

(1) You don't have to repay equity money
(2) Your business must usually be organized as a corporation to obtain equity money

You can obtain equity money from various sources, including:

- Sale of common stock in your firm
- Sale of warrants for your stock
- Exchange of your stock for other stock which you sell
- Sale of preferred stock in your firm

Equity means part ownership. So when you sell stock in your firm you do give up part of the ownership. But if you listen to your good friend, Ty Hicks, you:

- Can get equity money *without* losing control of your firm
- Can get up to $50-million without going into debt
- Can go back and get more money, if you need it

## How much OPM can you get

"Are you talking about a few hundred dollars, or a few thousand?" you ask. "After all, the amount can make a big difference in my business deals."

That's a fair question, from an intelligent reader. It shows that you're thinking.

The loan and equity sources you're about to learn about can provide you with anywhere from $5,000 to $50-million. Most of these sources prefer deals of more than $5,000 because on anything less the interest earnings are too small. Further, it costs just as much to process a $5,000 loan as a $50,000 loan! And while some of the lenders we'll soon tell you about will go over $50-million, the loans greater than $50-million are usually confined to governments of countries and similar large borrowers. So if $5,000 to $50-million will help you achieve your business goals, let's swing, man, swing!

Now, good friend, I want to give you a few tips on working with *all* lenders, be they:

- Banks
- Insurance companies
- Finance companies
- Venture-capital firms
- Private syndicates
- Stock underwriters making pre-offering loans

These *key* loan and equity success tips are: To get the best results from *any* lender, *never, never:*

(1) *Never* tell him you picked his name at random out of a list of lenders (this offends him).
(2) *Never* tell him you are "shopping" the loan application—that is, trying more than one lender (this makes him suspicious).
(3) *Never* tell him how poor you are—even if you are. (He only looks down on you and is much less likely to approve your application.)
(4) *Never* be afraid of any lender. He can't "eat" you, arrest you, fire you, kill you, or otherwise harm you. The most that he can do is say *no* to your application.
(5) *Never* become angry at a prospective lender. Though he says *no* today, he may call you tomorrow to say *yes.*

To get your money when you need it from lenders, *always, always:*

(1) Find out what *kinds* of loans a lender makes *before* you talk to him so you apply for the kind of loan he makes.
(2) Be friendly with the lender.
(3) Dress well when you appear for an interview.
(4) Type all applications and other documents.
(5) Speak only when spoken to.
(6) Be truthful and optimistic at all times.
(7) Be confident and assured.
(8) Seek grounds for agreement with the loan officer.
(9) Develop boldness and imagination.
(10) Use good government publications

### Develop boldness and imagination

In talking to thousands of BWB's all over the world I notice that many of them lack *boldness* and *imagination* when it comes to borrowing money. Now I'm not being critical of these BWB's—just observant and helpful.

Controlled and polite boldness can be one of your strongest assets when you're seeking OPM. Why? Because:

> Many lenders are meek rule-followers stuck in a fur-lined rut. When a bold and imaginative BWB comes along, the usual lender is so impressed that he's much more likely to make the loan the BWB asks for.

How can *you* develop boldness and imagination? Let's take these characteristics one at a time.

## BOLDNESS CAN PAY OFF

Boldness is an attitude based on a certain knowledge that if you're honest in *all* your business dealings (and you should *always* be honest) that:

- The most a prospective lender can do against you is say *no.*
- Determination *will* pay off—in time.
- Lenders are human—just like you and me.
- Fear of any lender *will* show through in every interview.
- Lenders abhor fear and often refuse a loan to a fearful applicant.
- And, as was once said, "The only thing we have to fear is fear itself." Further: "Optimism builds strength; pessimism leads to weakness."

To overcome fear, "dry run" every loan interview in advance—before you appear at the lender's office. Do this by listing the questions you think a lender might ask. Write down the answers you'll give to the questions. Ask yourself: "Do my answers make sense? Would *I* lend *my* money if someone gave these answers to *my* questions? Do my answers promise a deal that will make money for the lender?" (For that, after all, is why he's considering lending *you* the money.)

As a test of your answers, you may want to have a friend or relative ask you the lender's questions while playing the role of a lending officer. You then answer the questions. To hear what the interview sounds like, make a tape recording of it. Then you can play it back and listen to your answers. They'll quickly reveal whether you're relaxed or tense. If you *are* tense, you can take steps to improve your responses, reducing your nervousness.

During the actual loan interview in the lender's office, make notes of important points the lender brings up. Listen as much as possible, instead of talking. Try to learn as much as possible from *every* loan interview.

## IMAGINATION UNCOVERS HIDDEN MONEY

The easiest (and usually the smallest) kind of loan you can get is a *conventional loan.* And what kind of loan is this?

A conventional loan is one that fits the lender's formula for:

- Amount
- Purpose
- Duration
- Borrower qualifications
- Collateral

What we're saying, indirectly at least, is that the lender doesn't have to think about making such a loan to you because all the details fit a formula he worked out in advance.

To get a *BIG LOAN* you *must* be imaginative. You must:

- Come up with an eyecatching deal
- See *both* sides of every deal
- Offer the lender a big profit opportunity
- Prove to be a good credit risk

You can build *your* imaginative money powers in several ways, including:

- Reading about other deals people are offering to lenders. (The IWS monthly newsletter, *International Wealth Success,* is ideal for this purpose, and for many other purposes, such as finding hundreds of lenders.)
- Learning as much as you can about financial matters related to every type of business.
- Thinking up new ways of getting money you can put to work earning other money for you.

### Use good government aids

Here are a number of government aids which you might find helpful when you're searching for business funds.

## FROM THE SMALL BUSINESS ADMINISTRATION

### Free management aids:

How to Analyze Your Own Business, #46
Loan Sources in the Federal Government, #52
Choosing the Legal Structure for Your Firm, #80
Steps in Incorporating a Business, #111
The ABC's of Borrowing, #170
Is Your Cash Supply Adequate? #174
Financial Audits: A Tool for Better Management, #176
Borrowing Money from Your Bank, #11
How to Choose Your Banker Wisely, #39
Using Your Banker's Advisory Services, #68
Breaking the Barriers to Business Planning, #179
Providing Capital for Your Firm, #115
Helping the Banker Help You, #116
Bank Loan Limitations: Living Within Them, #158
Getting Money for Long-Term Growth, #138
Financing Export Sales, #149
What Kind of Money Do You Need? #150
Financial Facts Which Lenders Require, #164

### Small marketers' aids:

Checklist for Going Into Business, #71
Building Strong Relations with Your Bank, #107
Accounting Service for Small Firms, #126
Outwitting Bad Check Passers, #137
Understanding Truth in Lending, #139
Getting the Facts for Income-Tax Reporting, #144

See Chapter 1 for details on ordering these publications.

### It's easier than you think

People often moan and groan to me about how hard it is to get started in your own business these days. Yet I've met plenty of people around this world who actually carry one or more companies in their pocket and stocks and bonds in their attaché case.

Surely, if a person can run a company out of his hat, you can get yours going without a lot of complaining. Act, instead of worrying or looking for reasons for saying life is hard. Let me show you how your imaginative powers can overcome problems and get you the OPM you seek.

## Four unusual ways to get OPM

Four Beginning Wealth Builders needed money to get started in their own businesses. None knew the other. Yet each came up with a unique way of raising money for his beginning business. Here are the four ways.

### FLEXIBLE LOAN REPAYMENT

Wealth Builder No. 1: Wanted to borrow money with the under-standing that if the deal didn't work out he wouldn't have to repay. But if the deal was a success the lender would get a big share of the profits. Banks laughed at him; so did insurance firms, and other lenders. Using his mind, this BWB hit on the idea of borrowing through personal *investment advisers to wealthy people.* To wealthy people the potential loss on bad deals isn't a risk because what they lose they use to save taxes on other income. *Key: Loan repayment based on success of deal.* IWS gives new subscribers a free list of Personal Investment Advisers. Ask for their *Speculation Loan List* when you subscribe.

### ZERO-CASH FINANCING

Wealth Builder No. 2: Wanted to finance a fleet of rental sailboats for which he had *no* cash. So he advertised one-eighth ownership in each of three sizes of fiberglass sailboats. Enthusiasts bought up the ownership participations fast. The BWB got his rental boats; the eight owners can each use their boat one month a year free. This leaves four months a year for boat rental. Any extra income over the upkeep and other costs goes to the BWB. *Key: Financing for wanted income-producing property (the boats) obtained without putting up a cent.* (This is what I call a *Zero-Cash* technique).

## INTER-BUSINESS FINANCING

Wealth Builder No. 3: Wanted to open a mail-order business. He spent $300 on free New Product announcements which ran in 75 industrial magazines. These announcements generated $3,000 in sales. With his orders in hand, he was given long-term credit by his suppliers (270 days). This allowed him to ship, bill, and collect before he spent a cent on product. *Key: Big firms can help finance little firms using any of more than a dozen inter-business financing methods.*

## TAKEOVERS OF SICK FIRMS

Wealth Builder No. 4: Wanted to own his own mini-conglomerate (a collection of several firms) but had no cash. So he searched out sick firms (those that were bankrupt, or nearly so). He offered to take them off the owner's hands for no cash, and agreed to assume any and all pending debts. Result? He got his mini-conglomerate of five firms quickly and soon turned loss leaders into winners. *Key: Take over income-producers by taking on someone else's headaches.*

Now each of the above BWB's used his imagination to solve *his* money problems. *You can do the same!* For I firmly believe that as a BWB:

> In business, if you can imagine yourself doing something, you CAN ACTUALLY DO WHAT YOU IMAGINE!

So get started today:

- Using your imaginative powers
- Taking action on your thoughts
- Building your wealth
- Helping others help themselves
- Giving to charities of your choice
- Using your money to do good
- Developing a Rich Mental Attitude (RMA)

### Consider my methods

Beginning Wealth Builders (BWB's) are sometimes borrowing anywhere from $5,000 to $500,000 using the methods I recommend and the 25 to 100 lenders' names and addresses published in every issue of the monthly newsletter *International Wealth Success.* While you may not agree with my methods—and I respect you enormously for your disagreement—I most humbly must tell you that my methods have made me and a number of other people very wealthy. And I'd love to make you—and yours—millionaires too! I can do this for you if you follow my general hints and do what is good for yourself! So if you need anywhere up to $500,000 debt capital, or up to $50-million equity capital for your business, read on.

### Where to get your OPM

There are just two places to get your OPM, but each of them has many paths leading to it. The two places for you to get OPM for your business needs are:

| TYPE OF OPM | SOURCE |
|---|---|
| Debt Capital (loans) | Lenders of various kinds |
| Equity Capital (sale of stocks) | Stock buyers (usually the general public) |

Let's take a look at each source so you can put it to work for yourself to give you the business funds you need.

### How to borrow your way to a great fortune

You can, you know, *borrow* your way to great wealth! People (BWB's) do it every day of the year. So why can't you? I *know* you can because so many people who've read my books and other publications I recommend, *have* borrowed their way to enormous fortunes.

To *borrow* your way to a great fortune you must:

(1) Know who has money to lend
(2) Know the kinds of loans each lender makes
(3) Prepare a "selling" loan application
(4) Conduct a businesslike interview
(5) Close your deal so you get your money

If you know, and do, what these five items advise, I'm positive that you'll get the money you need quickly and easily. Let's see how.

## Know who has money to lend

Wanting and needing OPM is your first step to getting the money you need to put your business ideas into action. But many people never get beyond this first step because they don't know who's ready to lend them the money they need.

The best source of names and addresses of lenders of all kinds that I know of, which includes the names of:

- Banks
- Insurance companies
- Venture-capital firms
- Private lenders
- Mail-order lenders

is *Business Capital Sources* published by IWS Inc., P.O. Box 186, Merrick, N.Y. 11566, and priced at $15. This big book lists some 3,500 lenders who can provide you with the business money you need to get rich anywhere in the world. So your cost is less than half a penny a name!

## Know the kinds of loans each lender makes

Not knowing what kinds of loans a lender makes can:

- Waste your time
- Take the zip out of your ambition
- Cause you lost chances
- Get you down permanently

To show you what I mean, I'd like to tell you about a BWB who went wrong.

## DOOR KNOCKING DOESN'T ALWAYS PAY OFF

Clint K. is a BWB who wants to make big money in rental real estate. Following the advice in my five other best-selling money books,* Clint located several profitable apartment buildings. With their excellent profit and loss statements (called P&L's) in his hand, Clint called on six *commercial* banks in his southeastern city and applied for a $100,000 loan to take over several apartment houses. Each bank turned him down flat.

Clint was discouraged and beaten. Yet he wasn't ready to give up. As a last resort he gave me a ring on the telephone. "I'm sure you can't help me," he said. "But I thought I'd give you a ring, anyway."

"If you're so sure I can't help you, then don't waste my time and energy," I said, and hung up. (Anyone who starts with such a negative attitude can't command my attention or sympathies.)

Clint called back, full of apologies, saying "I realize now that you must be a positive thinker, or else you couldn't have done as much as you have in life. What have I done wrong?" (Clint then described his attempts to get real-estate funds at six different commercial banks.)

"You asked the wrong lender for the wrong kinds of funds for wrong purposes," I said. "Now listen to what I tell you, do as I say, and you'll get the money you need." Within a week Clint had borrowed the money he needed. Now here's what I told Clint.

## The world is full of lenders

Yes, the world *is* full of lenders—big ones, little ones, and in-between ones. And each lender, no matter what his size, has certain preferred and favorite types of loans which he makes, such as:

- Short-term loans
- Long-term loans

---

*How to Build a Second-Income Fortune in Your Spare Time; Smart Money Shortcuts to Becoming Rich; How to Start Your Own Business on a Shoestring and Make Up to $100,000 a Year; How to Borrow Your Way to a Great Fortune; Magic Mind Secrets for Building Great Riches Fast.* All are available from Parker Publishing Company, West Nyack, N.Y. 10994.

- Real-estate loans
- Commercial loans

If you fail to recognize this fact of business life, namely that:

> Every lender has a preferred type of loan which he
> makes faster and with less investigation

then you'll have real problems trying to get the business
OPM you need. For example, here are a few loan preferences
you'll often meet.

> Commercial banks (also called *business banks*) like to lend for *short*
> periods of time—seldom more than 3 years. So if you need a short-term
> loan—6 months, 1 year, or 2 years —apply at a commercial bank. But
> don't apply for a 20-year real-estate loan at a commercial bank; you'll
> be refused  just as Clint was because most commercial banks don't like
> long-term loans. Mortgage lenders, such as banks, finance companies,
> insurance companies, etc., are willing to lend real estate money for
> periods ranging from 5 to 40 years. So if you want a long-term
> real-estate loan, apply to a mortgage lender. (This is what I had Clint do
> and he got all the money he needed.)

To learn what kinds of loans lenders prefer, read your copy of
*Business Capital Sources:* How to Borrow the Business Money You
Need from 3,500 Carefully Selected Lenders, referred to earlier in
the chapter. For many of the lenders listed, you are shown what
types of loans they usually prefer. For some of the lenders listed
in *Business Capital Sources,* the preferred amounts which are
loaned are also listed. So, using this handy reference, you can
easily locate lenders throughout the world who might furnish the
OPM you need for your business deals.

### Prepare a "selling" loan application

In traveling all over the world for business purposes, I learn a
great deal about people, business deals, smart-money methods, and
so on. And one main fact that sticks in my mind from these travels
is this:

> Everyone, everywhere in the world, is selling something.
> So the better we are as salesmen, the easier our life will
> be.

Since—if you agree with me—everyone, everywhere, is selling
something, you are "selling" your loan application when you
apply for a loan from any lender. You have to "sell" the lender
the thought that it's good business for *him* to lend you *his* money.
Remember, at all times, this important fact:

> No lender ever lends you money because he wants to do
> you a favor. The only reason any lender ever lends
> money to anyone is because the loan promises to earn
> money for him!

Knowing this fact of business life, you can set out to "sell"
your application to the lenders you've selected from *Business
Capital Sources: How to Borrow the Business Money You Need
from 3,500 Carefully Selected Lenders.* To "sell" your application
you have to face the fact that any business loan application is sold
on the basis of:

(1) Appearance of the application
(2) Content of the application
(3) Your appearance during the personal interview

You will be successful in "selling" your loan application if you
take care of these three items *after* you've selected suitable
lenders. And if you have trouble picking lenders who'll lend you
the business money you need, I suggest you use the IWS *Venture
Capital Search* plan.

To use this plan, subscribe to *International Wealth Success,* the
monthly newsletter of wealth opportunities, for 2 years for $48,
and ask for their VCS loan application. Fill out the application
and return it to IWS. They'll take your applicaton and send it, free
of charge, to 12 carefully selected lenders, who could include:

- Banks
- Finance firms
- Mortgage lenders
- Venture-capital firms

By using this method, you have a better chance of getting the
business funds you need because you apply to lenders who are
looking for good loans to make. You can subscribe to IWS at P.O.
Box 186, Merrick, N.Y. 11566.

### Never pay "front" money

Some money finders, financial brokers, and other "helpers" in the business finance field will ask you to pay "front" money to get loans. And what's front money? *Front money is an advance (and usually non-refundable) fee charged by certain people and firms claiming they can get you business loans.*

Front money can range from a low of $50 to a high of $50,000, or more. Further, many so-called loan experts include a no-refund clause in the loan-search agreement they insist you sign.

Now take my advice. I've been "in the business of business" for many years. And my considered advice is:

> Never, never pay front money for any loan. You can pay
> a fee AFTER you receive your loan, if you wish, but
> never pay such a fee before your loan is approved.

Fast-buck operators will try to sell you on the need for a fee in advance because, they say, they have to:

- Write up application forms
- Mail your application to lenders
- Meet their overhead (phone, light, heat, and other operating costs)
- Spend time on your deal

All of this is true. But unless they're willing to take a chance on getting *you your loan,* don't do business with these people. Some fast-buck operators are in just one business—that of collecting front money. Don't fall for their lines. You can find plenty of no-front-money leads every month in IWS. So why pay when you don't have to?

### Make a good impression on every lender

To impress *any* lender and "sell" your application sooner and with less pain (yes, borrowing *can* be painful, at times) be sure to:

- *Type* your loan application, if you can. Handwritten loan applications are seldom approved for loans over $5,000.

- Use a *printed* letterhead when you send your application to the lender.
- Fill out *all* spaces that apply to you.
- Be *neat* and *precise* in all your correspondence.

Remember this important fact about your loan application:

> When the Loan Approval Committee is making its decision, the only document it has is your loan application. So "you" are your application. Be sure "you" look good.

Many lenders will ask you to appear personally for an interview. (Where you'd prefer to handle all details by mail, use the mail-order lenders listed in *Business Capital Sources*.) When you appear for a loan interview:

(1) Wear suitable business clothing.
(2) Speak quietly and politely.
(3) Supply whatever data you are asked for.
(4) Try to appeal to the loan officer's interests.
(5) Convince the loan officer that doing business with you would be good business for him and his firm.

Thus, getting a business loan is both a business and personality deal. You can't get the loan on either element alone. Both aspects enter the preparation and approval of your business loan papers.

### Conduct a businesslike loan interview

To get your loan story across, conduct a businesslike loan interview. In interviews where you appear in person:

(1) Don't smoke, unless the loan officer does.
(2) Don't sprawl all over his desk, chair, or couch.
(3) Don't talk to him while he's writing or on the telephone—he can think of only one thing at a time.
(4) If he asks you who recommended his bank or firm, tell him a highly reputable financial consultant recommended his organization as being outstanding for the type of loan you are seeking. And who is the financial consultant doing the

recommending? It's either I or *Business Capital Sources,* whichever you'd prefer.

You *can* get the business funds you seek—if you look long enough and far enough. Just recently, a BWB who was starting a new magazine applied to 60 lenders for a $100,000 start-up loan. The 60th lender stamped his application *Approved* and the next day he picked up his $100,000 check. "Now even if I spent two hours at each lender, which I didn't, Ty, I'd still be making about $1,000 an hour!" said this BWB to me after he got his loan. "I'll work for wages like that any day!"

Another BWB needed $120,000 for a second mortgage to take over an income-producing property. He decided to get his money by writing to second mortgage lenders instead of visiting them in person. This BWB wrote to 352 mortgage lenders. The first 351 refused to lend him the money but the 352nd said *YES!* And instead of getting $120,000, this BWB was able to borrow $135,000, meaning that the deal worked out thus:

| | |
|---|---|
| Price of apartment building | $600,000 |
| Existing first mortgage | $500,000 |
| Cash required | $100,000 |
| Second mortgage | $135,000 |
| Money left for closing costs | $ 35,000 |
| Closing costs | $ 15,000 |
| Money left for BWB | $ 20,000 |

Thus, this BWB *mortgaged out*—that is got $20,000 for taking over an income-producing property that will give him a return of over $5,000 per month, free and clear! But to get this deal going he had to write 352 letters. "Was it worth it?" you ask. I think so—don't you?

Although I hope you don't have to visit 60 lenders, or write to 352, to get your business loan, keep in mind the fact that:

> Borrowing methods can be as changeable as the weather
> because the money supply varies every day.

Knowing this fact of business life, your best approach to get the money you need is to keep trying—after you've picked your potential lenders.

### Close the interview—with your money

Try to end every loan interview, whether in person or by mail:

(1) With your money in hand
(2) Friends with your lender

Money in hand is, of course, the goal of your loan search. So when you end the interview with your money in hand, you've achieved your goal.

But there's another important fact about borrowing business funds that is worth keeping in mind, namely:

> Once a lender loans you money, he wants to see you succeed so that he'll be repaid his money, and you'll want to borrow some more of his money in the future.

So it will pay you—both in terms of a more cordial relationship today and the potential for more money tomorrow—to:

- Be friendly with *every* lender
- Maintain a cordial politeness towards lenders
- Be a gentleman or lady at all times
- Remember the lender's name and have him remember yours

You *can* go back to the money well again and again if you carefully plan your campaign and then *work* your plan! To prove this is so, I'll soon give you some real-life examples of how other BWB's got the business money they needed quickly and easily. But first let's take a look at unusual sources of business money.

### Get your money from offbeat sources

When considering OPM, most BWB's think of banks as their main source of business funds. While I am very fond of banks and make much use of their services in my various businesses, I know that some ambitious BWB's have found that banks:

- Can have very strict loan requirements
- May deal only with established firms

- Sometimes require several cosigners
- Are sometimes slow in approving loans

Now I'm not criticizing banks. Instead, I'm repeating some of the complaints I've had from *some* BWB's about *some* banks. What we all must remember is that:

> Banks are one of your keys to success in building your fortune. So always be friendly with your banker. But at the same time, keep alert to unusual sources of business money.

Unusual sources of business money you might consider include:

- Overseas lenders
- Government capital sources
- Venture-capital firms
- Import-export dealers
- Mortgage lenders
- Private lenders
- Inter-business lenders

To borrow money or get credit from lenders such as those listed above, you have to know their names and addresses, and how to do business with them. You'll find the names and addresses of many of these lenders in the following books: (1) *Business Capital Sources;* (2) *SBIC Directory and Small Business Handbook;* (3) *Handbook of Successful Borrowing of Money for Business;* (4) *Inter-Business Financing;* (5) *How to Get Venture Capital;* and (6) *Worldwide Riches Opportunities,* Volumes 1 and 2. All are obtainable from IWS Inc., at the prices listed at the back of this book.

## Borrow the most from each unusual source

Almost anyone can go out and borrow $1,000, $2,000, or even $5,000. What I want *you* to be able to borrow is $50,000, $100,000, or $300,000—if your business needs this amount of money. To get sums of these magnitudes, you need good guidelines.

## DON'T SCATTER YOUR EFFORTS

Earl C. needed such guidance to borrow $250,000 to take over a plush apartment house in his city. In his first flush of enthusiasm, Earl applied to every lender whose name he came across. But he was turned down for various reasons, including:

- The amount you want is too small
- The amount you want is too large
- We don't make real-estate loans
- You don't have enough collateral
- Your collateral is the wrong kind
- You're too young to borrow
- You're too old to borrow

These reasons for rejecting your loan application are typical of what you can expect when you apply for business funds in an unplanned manner, without guidance. But get a little guidance from trained people and you can soon have lenders knocking on your door, pleading with you to accept their loans.

One good source of guidance is the IWS Venture Capital Search (VCS) loan plan. To get this guidance all you need do is subscribe to the monthly newsletter *International Wealth Success* for two years ($48), or renew your subscription for another year if you are already a subscriber. Once your subscription payment is received, IWS sends you its specially designed VCS loan application. You fill it out and return it to IWS which:

- Carefully selects 12 qualified lenders for you
- Types 12 special envelopes for your loan application
- Sends one copy of your application to each lender
- Returns any extra copies of your loan application to you

To get your VCS application with a two-year subscription to IWS, send $48 to IWS Inc., P.O. Box 186, Merrick, N.Y. 11566. Your loan application will be processed the same day it is received giving you a fast turnaround. You do *not* have to supply confidential data to get your loan approved.

## Get money that needn't be paid back

Every lender is in business to make money on the money he lends you. But every lender also wants to get his money back! Why? Because he's not in the charity business. Instead, he's in the business of lending you money for a profit. So:

> When you borrow money you MUST make regular repayments on some time basis—monthly, semi-annually, or annually. But you MUST repay.

You will often find that your repayments are a burden on you and your business. Why? Because loan repayments can:

- Cut into your cash flow
- Stop new deals you're trying to work
- Over-burden a new business

For these reasons, many BWB's long for a way to raise business capital free of regular repayments. "Is there any way this can be done?" they often ask. "There sure is," I reply. "You just 'go public.' "

When you *go public* you, through your *corporation:*

- Sell some stock in your corporation to the public
- Get money—from $100,000 to $50-million or more
- Need not repay the money

"But must *I* sell the stock myself?" you ask. "I hate to sell people anything."

## It's quicker than you think

No, you needn't sell the stock yourself. You can have an *underwriter* (a firm that sells stock) do that for you. To answer some questions I know you'll have, I'll tell you the following about going public.

- *The underwriting cost* is usually 15 percent, or less, of the offering, and is paid from the proceeds (what the public pays) of the offering. *You don't put up a cent!* Thus, on a $500,000 offering, the cost would be about $75,000.

- *You don't give up* control of your company when you go public. There are plenty of simple ways for you to keep essentially complete control of your firm.
- *You get your corporate money fast* when you go public—usually within 90 days, or less, after the offer is first made. (Often the underwriter will lend you money to tide you over during the offering period.)
- *Your firm need not have made a sale,* profit, or *any* other income before you go public. This means that brand-new, unproven firms can go public easily and quickly. (Of course, it's easier to go public if your firm has a sales and business history.)
- You can use the money from a public offering for any number of purposes—such as:

  - Pay off debts
  - Pay salaries
  - Buy supplies
  - Pay rent
  - Buy real estate
  - Employee expense accounts

### Learn how to go public

You can take your own corporation public—if you want to—if you're an elected officer of the corporation. But I don't recommend this do-it-yourself approach; there are too many traps for the unwary. Instead, I recommend that you get good advice from a qualified attorney.

If you want to learn how to take a corporation public, including how to prepare the various documents you need, I suggest that you buy the IWS *Financial Broker-Finder-Business Broker Program.* Costing $99.50, this excellent Program shows you exactly how to take any firm public. It also gives full data on becoming a highly paid finder and business broker. Four handsome, diploma-like certificates are included with your Program.

### How you can get the funds you need

Hundreds and hundreds of small firms go public every year. And most of these use the Regulation A method which currently allows the firm to sell $500,000 or less of securities without having to make expensive financial projections. You can (and should) make the money plans yourself.

Can a firm just be starting and still go public? Yes; plenty are new, untried firms. These are called *promotional-type* firms, while companies that are already operating are called *operational-type* firms.

In recent years I've watched thousands of companies go public. And BWB's have done the following as part of this march to the public for interest-free, non-repayable funds:

- $300,000 obtained for a promotional start-up firm with *no* underwriter—the company officers sold their own stock, saving about $45,000 in fees.
- A "blank-check" type real-estate investment trust sold $10-million worth of securities to the public and didn't make its first investment (of about $500,000) until almost a year later. (A *blank-check* deal is one in which the firm does not state which properties it will buy with the money it gets—only the kind—apartment houses, motels, and the like.)
- $5.2-million raised for a start-up (or new) company which had not yet made one sale.
- $1,500,000 obtained by a 2-year-old computer firm which was just starting to show a profit.

## There's plenty of money for you

Yes, good friends, you *can* borrow *your* way to great wealth. To prove it to yourself, just start using some of the methods I've given you in this chapter. Or improve on these methods, using your own powers of imagination. Just be sure to write me and tell me how well your methods work! I'll put them in my next wealth book.

### POINTS TO REMEMBER

- You *can* borrow your way to a great fortune—people do it every day of the year.
- Today smart people use borrowed money to build their wealth.
- Borrowing is *in,* is decent, is sensible.
- You must know who lends what, for how long, and for which uses.
- Your best salesman can be your loan application.
- Be friendly with *every* lender.

- Develop boldness and imagination to get your money from unusual sources.
- Try to get no-interest, non-repayable money whenever you can.
- Don't listen to people who tell you that a new start-up company can't go public. Plenty of firms have, and are doing, exactly that today!

9

# Build Your Riches
# Starting with Zero Cash

People often ask me: "What's the fastest way to get rich when you don't have any capital, credit, collateral, company, corporation, or convincing ideas which other people will finance with *their* money?" I have what I believe is the perfect answer to this question. (At least the answer is perfect for *most* people in *most* circumstances.)

This chapter gives you that answer in a quick, concise form. By reading this chapter you'll quickly learn how anyone—from beginner to bankrupt—can build a fast fortune in his own business, starting with zero cash, no credit, and no collateral, while using other people's money.

Now before I show you how to get rich using the method described in the answer to the above question, I want to qualify the method. Four businessmen I know of began with this method when they were $2,000 in debt. Within two years, they were worth $1-million. Ten years later, they owned a number of businesses having a total value of over $400-million. If you call that getting rich fast, then read on to learn how you, and others, can use this secret and magic method.

### Seven steps show success secrets

The riches success method which you're about to learn is called the HICKS FAST FORTUNE NO-CASH, NO-CREDIT, NO-COLLATERAL WAY TO WEALTH (FASFOR). This FASFOR method has seven outstanding steps or features for you, namely:

1. NO CASH needed
2. Fast assets buildup
3. Immediate cash income
4. Long-term debt payoff possible
5. Improved credit rating possible
6. Power over people
7. Instant wealth can be yours

Let's take a quick look at each of these features from *your* standpoint to see how you can use it to make a *fast* big win in the money game.

### *Forget Your Money Worries*

1. *No cash needed.* To use the FASFOR method, you don't need a penny of investment money. You will, however, need about $25 for postage and phone calls. This is such a small amount that it is almost negligible. Further, if you live in a large city you can walk from one place of business to another, thereby saving the $25 for postage and telephone. But the important point in all this is:

> Using the FASFOR method you can take over wealth-producing assets with NO CASH investment.

### *Move Ahead Quickly*

2. *Fast assets buildup.* An asset is any tool, machine, building, factory, or other facility used in business to produce income. Assets are worth plenty of money. For instance, you can pay $1-million for a big machine tool—such as a lathe or milling machine—and still not have it making money for you until after you've spent another $100,000 to have the machine installed. So you see, if you can take over an asset with no cash down, you have

obtained something of value at no cost to yourself! And if you can take over a lot of assets in a hurry, you can get rich fast, which is the whole objective of the FASFOR method.

### Get Your Cash Now

3. *Immediate cash income.* Let's say today is Monday, the first day you put your FASFOR method into action. By Friday of the *same* week you could have in your hand a check for anywhere between $1,000 and $1-million, depending on what kind of deal you went into. While waiting from Monday to Friday makes your cash a little less than "immediate," it's close enough to immediate to allow use of the word. What's more, you can get this money WITHOUT putting up your personal credit rating, or collateral. In fact, one of the secrets of success of the FASFOR method is:

> You use the credit and assets of others to build your fortune. You can start with the worst credit rating in the world (such as being bankrupt) and still make an enormous fortune. So forget about a bad credit rating from this moment on!

### Take All the Time You Need

4. *Long-term debt payoff possible.* If you go out to borrow money on a business signature loan, you'll usually have to pay the money back in 36 months, or less. Most other loans you can get today—business or other kinds—will run for not more than 60 months, or perhaps even less. This means you can be saddled with heavy debt repayments, making your life difficult.

With the FASFOR method, you can take 10 years, or longer, to pay off your business debts. This means that you'll have smaller debt payments, allowing you more profit from your business.

### Build for Your Future

5. *Improved credit rating possible.* In the FASFOR system you use the credit rating and assets of *others,* instead of your own. And, in most cases I know of, the BWB (Beginning Wealth Builder) using the FASFOR method winds up with a better credit rating than he started with! Remember:

There's no better way to improve your credit rating than

to get some solid assets behind it. The FASFOR method
does just that for you.

### Expand Your Abilities

6. *Power over people.* When you use the FASFOR method you
become the boss. You get cash capital without personal credit
or collateral. As the boss of a growing empire you can exert
enormous power over people—men and women. With the money
reins in your hands, you acquire great personal power. People
will:

- Obey your orders
- Work for you day and night
- Be more willing to help you
- Become your personal friend
- Go places with you

### Don't Delay—Act Now

7. *Instant wealth can be yours.* I know of no other faster or
surer way for a BWB to go from a condition of:

| | | |
|---|---|---|
| • No capital | | • Capital in the bank |
| • No credit | | • Top credit rating |
| • No assets | | • Tangible assets |
| • No collateral | *TO* | • Adequate collateral |
| • No business | | • Good business |
| • No borrowing ability | | • High borrowing power |

than the FASFOR method. If I've convinced you of the validity,
speed, and sureness of the FASFOR method, then climb aboard
with me, good friend, while I show you how to make a fast
fortune without collateral or credit.

## Learn the zero-cash method

Your zero-cash FASFOR method is very simple—so simple that
you can use it in any number of businesses. Here are the key steps
you can take in any business by using the FASFOR method:

1. Find a business that's in deep financial trouble—that is, a
   business that is about to go broke or bankrupt—in other
   words, it's sick.

2. Get the money facts about the business—how much it owes, to whom, what the annual income is, how much the plant (factory, machinery, buildings, other equipment) is worth.
3. Decide how much—if any—cash the business is worth.
4. Make an offer to buy the business.
5. Close the deal if the terms are suitable to yourself.
6. See the creditors—that is the people or firms the business owes money to.
7. Arrange a reduced-money, extended time offer to the creditors to pay off the debts.
8. Close the credit deal.
9. Sell off some of the assets of the business.
10. Promote and sell the product or services for which the business is known.
11. Expand your holdings.
12. Diversify your activities.

Now I know that these 12 steps may be a shock to some people. "It has to be easier than that," they say. Really, friends, the FASFOR method *is* easier to use than the above 12 steps make it sound. To see that this is so, let's take a look at each step to learn how *you* can use the steps, and the FASFOR method, to build great riches fast.


**Find a business that's in trouble**

The key to the FASFOR method is the finding of a sick business that you can take over for NO CASH DOWN, or for very little cash down—say less than $100. "But what kinds of businesses can someone get for no cash down?" you ask. Plenty, such as:

- Manufacturing—products, textiles, furniture
- Service—personal, commercial
- Raw materials—mining, lumber
- Real estate—rental housing
- Many, many others

"I'm convinced, at least partly," you say. "Now how, and

where, do I find such a business?" That's just the question I want to answer here.

You find a no-cash-down business by *looking for it!* Such a business won't come looking for you—unless you:

- Let people know you're looking
- Go out and *look*
- Get price quotations
- Study details of proposed deals

To get complete details of businesses for sale in your area:

(1) Contact local business brokers
(2) Advertise free of charge in *International Wealth Success*
(3) Check with local real-estate agents who also handle business sales
(4) Use the accompanying list of business brokers for a nation-wide source of businesses for sale

## Important facts for you

Now you must remember several key facts about the FASFOR technique. These facts are:

(A) You are looking for "sick" businesses—that is those that:

- Owe money to people
- Are losing money
- Don't have much promise

(B) You are doing the seller a favor when you take over the "sick" business

(C) The seller will be delighted to "get out from under" his bills and problems

(D) Your profits will come from several sources related to this "sick" business, including:

- Sale of some assets
- Sale of products or services
- Reducing operating costs

Don't make the mistake of thinking that cash-free business takeovers are hard to find. There are plenty of these cash-free takeovers available all around the world. All you have to do is keep your eyes open. Read the:

- Business ads in your local paper
- Classified ads in industrial magazines
- *International Wealth Success* newsletter

Sometimes you may even find a business that you can take over without any cash down which will have cash in the bank! So, after signing a few papers, you walk away as owner of a business and you have money in the bank! Truly, good friend of mine, it can be done! Could anyone ask for a sweeter deal? Once you've found the business, you're ready to check out the money facts on the business.

### Get the money data on the business

The purpose of any business is to earn an acceptable profit for its owners. A good business can do plenty of other things for you, such as keeping you supplied with new Cadillacs, a big yacht, a plush office, pretty secretaries, and other luxuries. But ultimately the name of the game is profit for the owners. A business that doesn't show a profit isn't worth much to anyone, unless its operation is just a hobby for someone.

To get the details on the profits of a business, you must know the money facts about the business, or the:

- Annual total (also called gross) sales
- Cost of materials
- Labor costs
- Selling costs
- Overhead costs (rent, light, heat, phone)
- Tax expenses
- Annual profit or loss

You can get these money facts from several sources:

(1) Income-tax returns of the firm
(2) The account books of the firm

(3) A certified statement from an accountant
(4) Data published in the firm's annual report

## Don't make beginners' mistakes

Now don't be fooled by these figures. Most beginners avidly look for the net profits earned by the firm in recent years. Actually, if the firm were earning a good net profit, it wouldn't be for sale. It's the firms that *are not* earning a net profit that you're interested in! So look for the following facts about the firm you're thinking of taking over:

(1) How much money the firm owes
(2) Whom the money is owed to
(3) Book value of the plant and equipment
(4) Actual value of any inventory
(5) Actual value of the plant and equipment

Remember this fact about every takeover you're considering:

> The book value of a company may be low, its debts high, but if the actual value of the inventory and assets is higher, you have a potential winner.

So don't be fooled by the obvious—dig deep while sluggards sleep. Look for hidden values under the figures you've studied. Thus, you will often find firms with actual values much greater than their debts, yet their owners are completely unaware of this! Sounds crazy, I know, but it sure is true. Look around at a few firms and you'll see that what I say is actually so.

## Decide how much the firm is worth

You're going to make an offer for the firm you've studied. In most cases this offer will be *zero cash*. But just because zero cash is involved, you should not take shortcuts to save time or energy.

Once you take over this firm it will be yours and you'll have to run it. So you don't want to "pay" too much for it in the form of:

(1) Promissory notes, Figure 9-1
(2) A percentage of the future profits
(3) Shares of stock

or in any other type of "paper."

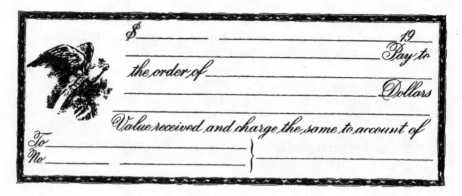

**Figure 9-1**

**How "paper" can make you rich**

Now note this fact about "paper." A *promissory note* is nothing more than a slip of paper about 3 inches high and 8 inches long which you sign, and with which you promise to pay the *holder* of the note a certain amount of money (say $500) on a certain date (say June 1st). The seller of the business looks upon the note as money. The usual interest you pay on a promissory note is 6 percent simple interest, which is tax deductible by the business, if the business guarantees the note, or by yourself if you stand behind the note. (You may, of course, have to pay a higher rate of interest to the seller.)

To decide how much a firm is worth to you, take these steps:

(1) Figure the "quick asset" value—that is how much you could get by selling all the firm's assets for cash. (If you don't

know the quick asset value of the firm, make a conservative guess.)

(2) Value the firm at one-quarter to one half your estimate of the quick asset value.

When placing a value on any business in the FASFOR method:

> Figure how much you could lose on the deal before you
> figure how much you could make.

The potential loss figure can shake you up and make you take a clearer look at the deal BEFORE you make any offers. My wide experience in business has taught me:

> Whenever possible, deal with trouble before it occurs;
> then you'll have fewer problems and you'll be readier to
> handle those problems that do occur.

So, as a general guide, value a firm, or real estate, at one-quarter to one-half of its *quick cash value.*

## Make an offer for the business

Your offer is an important step in taking over any business. And since you will be making a *no-cash* offer, your offer must be carefully planned and thought through. Using the 25 percent or 50 percent of value basis that I recommended, make your offer with these terms:

(1) *NO* cash down
(2) Promissory notes for the payments for the business
(3) Ten-year payoff for the notes

Be ready to offer concessions if the above terms are not accepted. The concessions you might offer are:

(1) Profit-sharing in addition to notes
(2) Five-year payoff of notes
(3) Shares of stock in the business

And now let's see how this offer might work in a real-life situation.

Let's say that you're interested in taking over a manufacturing business which you've estimated has a quick value of $500,000, using a 50 percent basis. This means you believe you could sell the assets of the business for $1-million.

## Many owners want out

But the business has been losing money in recent years and the owners want to sell it. You think you can turn the business around and make it profitable. To turn the loss into a profit will take at least two years, you think. During this time, you'll be earning a nice salary of $75,000 a year as president of the company. To protect yourself against future problems, here's what you offer, and why:

| OFFER | REASON |
|---|---|
| 1. No cash down | 1. You don't have any cash |
| 2. No note payments for first two years | 2. You may need this long to earn a profit |
| 3. $500,000 on promissory notes | 3. This is the value you place on the business |
| 4. All company debts will be paid by the firm | 4. This is your "carrot" offer to the owners; you'll see later why it can work wonders |

## Be ready to change your offer

Now don't expect this offer to be accepted exactly as you make it. Few sellers will accept every one of your terms. So be prepared for some wheeling and dealing. But be sure you are the winning dealer and:

• Don't pay any cash
• Delay note payments for at least one year
• Insist on using promissory notes

With this approach, you should be able to take over the business quickly and easily. Now note this fact:

The entire FASFOR method hinges on NO cash down, delayed payments, and the use of promissory notes. So

don't vary from this approach until you've gained some
experience.

Another fact that some BWB's overlook is this. The promissory
notes you sign will give you credit faster than any bank or other
lender will. Also, the seller of a business will seldom check out
your credit rating before allowing you to take over his business by
using promissory notes. So the FASFOR technique can help you
get around a poor credit rating while putting you in the big
money! You could have been bankrupt at one time, but you can
still sign takeover notes and get credit!

### Close the deal quickly

Wheel and deal to get the seller to accept your offer quickly.
Once he says OK to your offer, get a lawyer to work up the sales
agreement. The usual terms of such an agreement are well known
by lawyers. While you might buy a business alone, I strongly
recommend that you *never buy a business without the advice of a
competent attorney.* For, as a famous lawyer once said to me:
"The people who get into legal trouble are those who try to do
things themselves. Spend a little money at the start of a deal and
you'll seldom have any legal problems later on!"

Keep the following facts in mind whenever you are starting,
negotiating, or closing a takeover deal:

(1) Have an attorney
(2) *Never* sign any papers without consulting your attorney first
(3) Put up *NO* cash—pay the attorney out of the business you
     take over
(4) Be ready for shouts, screams, and tears at the closing
(5) Keep your cool—don't let any part of the deal upset you
(6) Be ready for the worst and you'll get the best

### See the firm's creditors

A creditor is a person or organization to whom *your* firm owes
money. And since *you* now *own* the firm, you also *owe* the money
the firm owes to its creditors. It is a characteristic of almost every

sick firm that it owes money—and usually lots of money. If the firm didn't owe money you probably couldn't take it over with no cash down. Since *you* now owe the money, *you* must do something about repaying these debts. Here's what to do.

(1) Call, or write, each creditor and explain that you've just taken over the business
(2) Set up an appointment with each creditor
(3) Visit the creditors
(4) Explain that you've just taken over the business
(5) Convince the creditor of your desire to pay off *all* the debts of the business as quickly as possible
(6) Explain that the business has NO cash at the moment but that you hope to have some in six months to a year

With these points made, you are now ready to make the next big move in your FASFOR method. Here it is.

### Make a reduced-money, extended-time offer

Let's say that your firm owes creditor *A* $50,000 for materials. The debt has dragged on for more than a year and creditor *A* has little hope of ever seeing a penny of his $50,000. You visit him and tell him that you want to repay as much as possible of this debt.

"But, we're very short of cash," you remark, "so the best I can promise to pay is 30 to 50 percent of what the firm owes. And things are so tough that we'll have to pay you over a ten-year period." Thus, you've made your offer, namely:

*Reduced-payment* of $15,000 to $25,000 on a $50,000 debt
*Extended period* of 10 years, starting one year from now

Most creditors will jump at such an offer because it promises them 30 to 50 percent of their money in place of *no* money at all. Wouldn't you rather have some money in place of none, if you were the creditor?

Once the creditor accepts your offer, send him a letter, or have your attorney send him a letter worded as follows:

Dear Mr._____:

It was a pleasure to meet you on __(date)__ to discuss the $50,000 debt owed you by the _(name)_Corporation.

As we agreed at that meeting, _(name)_ will settle this debt for the sum of $25,000 to be paid in monthly installments over a 10-year period beginning one year from today.

To signify your acceptance of this offer, please sign both copies of this letter in the space provided below and return one copy to us for our files.

Very truly yours,

_(name)_ Corporation
J. Doe, President

I (we) hereby agree to the settlement amount and repayment timing specified above.

_____                    _____
(name; signed)                                              (title)

_____
(date)


Follow this procedure with each creditor and you'll have:

(1) Reduced your firm's debt by 50 to 70 percent*
(2) Extended the payoff time by 11 years
(3) Obtained complete relief from debt for one year
(4) Placed your firm in an excellent economic position

Now let's pause for just a moment to see where you stand. You:

- Own the firm
- Have cut your firm's debts
- Are free from debt payments for a year
- Can now start making money
- Look like a good guy or gal to the creditors
- Have done all this with NO CASH!

---

*Of course, if you think you can pay off *ALL* debts in their *FULL* amount, you should do so.

## Sell off some assets

Up to this point you've been working strictly for love. Your future was a promise. Now we're ready to make your future become today!

The firm you bought with no cash down has some assets, such as:

- Machinery
- Inventory of merchandise or raw materials
- Real estate
- Patents, copyrights, or licenses
- Distribution rights

These assets are worth money to you—*cash money*. What you have to do is:

(1) List all the assets the firm owns
(2) Place a value on each asset
(3) Advertise the assets
(4) Negotiate a cash sale

Now you usually don't want to sell (also called *liquidate*) all the firm's assets. You want to keep some of the assets to allow you to continue the firm's business. The only time you *might* want to sell all the firm's assets is when you could get *more cash* for the assets than the total of what the firm owes. This *can* be done, and *is* sometimes done. Businessmen call it the *bailing out technique*. By selling the assets you get enough money to pay off the firm's debts and walk away with cash in your pocket.

Let's say, however, that you just want to sell *half* the assets of the firm. Your list of half the assets shows that you have, ready for quick sale:

| NAME OF ASSET | PROBABLE SALE VALUE |
|---|---|
| Production machinery | $ 80,000 |
| Real estate (2 lots) | 30,000 |
| Patent on machine | 40,000 |
| Distributorship franchise | 100,000 |
| Total estimated sale value | $250,000 |

Thus, if you could sell all these assets you could quickly raise $250,000 CASH! Since these are only half the assets of the firm, you will still have a production capability after you sell these assets.

## Don't worry about "book value"

Now you may ask: "But what about the book value of the assets?" The *book value* of an asset is the amount of money an asset (such as a machine or building) is listed as being worth on the firm's account books. The book value is supposed to show the depreciated value of the asset. But in most sick firms there is little relation between the book value of the assets and the price you can sell these assets for in the open market. So from a fortune-building point of view you will usually ignore book value unless your accountant screams at you to take the book value into account.

Let's say that by advertising in *International Wealth Success, The Wall Street Journal*, and *The New York Times*, you get $240,000 cash for the assets listed above. This is the firm's money and it will usually be tax-free because there is seldom a profit on such sales. You can use the money from the sale of the firm's assets to:

- Pay your salary
- Pay yourself special fees
- Pay your expense account costs
- Pay other people
- Pay for new equipment for the firm

Using these and other funds from the company you can have a:

- Big auto (Cadillac or Rolls Royce)
- Corporate yacht or boat
- Private company jet or prop plane
- Hotel suite for relaxing and entertaining
- Complete expense account
- Secretaries on call at any hour
- Electronic equipment of all types
- Travel to anywhere in the world
- Country and yacht club membership

Thus, you can live the life of a top executive and be the envy of all your friends. What's more, as president of your own firm you:

- Can give the orders
- Can ask the questions
- Can demand good performance
- Can be the leader

You will have power and mastery over the lives of others—both men and women. By using this power wisely and carefully, you can help build the fortunes and careers of many people. This can give you a good, warm feeling inside yourself which money can't buy. And having the niceties of life paid for by your firm allows you to expand your personality and help others. You'd be surprised how much easier it is to be nice when *you* have all the money you need to satisfy your wants and desires!

**Try selling off some inventory**

You can also sell off any excess inventories—finished products or raw materials—your firm has on hand. Sale of these items can generate more quick cash for you which you can use for the same purposes listed before. Although the cash you receive for inventories seldom equals the usual sale price of finished items, you can often sell inventories faster and with less effort than needed for machinery or real estate. Thus, plenty of inventories are sold on the basis of one phone call!

At the end of this chapter you find a list of some dealers in inventories and related items who may be able to help you sell off the inventories of the firm you buy. These names and addresses were culled from the monthly newsletter *International Wealth Success,* whose motto is: *IWS—Your fastest way to a great personal fortune.*

**Use the sell-off technique to catch quick wealth**

Parts of the company you take over may be worth more money to your competitors than they are to you. Knowing this, you

*Available for $24 per year for 12 big monthly issues from IWS Inc., P.O. Box 186, Merrick, N.Y. 11566.

might *sell-off* (i.e., sell) a division, department, or other part of your firm. This can put quick money in your pocket in the form of:

- Cash
- Stocks or bonds
- Other assets

So consider selling off one or more parts of your firm. You can profit quickly and pull your firm out of debt with unusual swiftness.

Another approach to the sell-off technique is the setting up of separate firms, using various divisions or departments of your company as the basis of these firms. The theory behind this approach is:

> The public will value more highly (that is, pay more for) the stock of several companies than they will the stock of a single company.

Using this technique you can split up your firm into several smaller firms and sell the stock of each to the public. (For full details on going public with a small firm, see the IWS *Financial Broker-Finder-Business Broker-Consultant Program.* Costing only $99.50, it shows you exactly how to sell stock to the public, under the guidance of your attorney.)

Plenty of small, and large, firms have made big profits selling off parts of their business or selling stock to the public. You can do the same and make a takeover your source of a great fortune.

The firm you took over has some product or service (or both) to sell. Now is the time to start planning to go out and aggressively sell that product or service. (You will seldom do the selling yourself; instead your sales force will do the job for you.) But before your sales force starts selling, you want to cut costs to the lowest possible level. You can cut costs by:

- Reducing your payroll
- Better buying practices
- Closing rented space
- Getting more output from each worker

Cutting costs can be very painful to you and your company staff because it usually means firing people. Many of these people may be long-time employees of the firm. For instance, in a recent takeover of a sick firm, 40 of the 80 employees in the engineering department had to be let go. There was plenty of crying and gnashing of teeth amongst the long-term staff in the department when the layoffs were announced. Yet a year later, everyone in the engineering department quickly admits that:

- More work is being done by 40 men than the 80 men did
- Each worker is more efficient
- Costs are less than half of what they were
- Salaries are higher than before

I've seen, and been active in, hundreds of business takeovers. And in every case of a sick company, cutting costs had excellent results. True, you hurt some feelings when you cut costs. But running a business solely on the basis of feelings is seldom profitable. What you have to do is to consider people's feelings while trying to reduce costs. Then you cut costs as much as possible while hurting the fewest people.

Often you can rehire people at a later date when the results of your cost cuts have made your business boom. At that time people will love you for your cost-cutting efforts!


### Go now to market

With your firm slimmed down and costs at a low level, you're ready to sell your product or service throughout the world. This is where you can take a sick firm and "turn it around" to make it a profitable, swinging firm that will:

- Pay you a large current income
- Increase in value, day by day
- Be ready for sale at a fat capital-gains profit
- Build your fortune quickly

To make your firm earn high profits, take these steps:

(1) Isolate the items or services producing the largest profit per sale
(2) Have your salesmen concentrate on the high profit producers

(3) Ignore, from a sales-producing viewpoint, the loss producers—they just waste time and energy

(4) Try to sell off to other firms your loss producers and slow products; other firms may be glad to get them!

(5) Introduce new products carefully

(6) Figure what you can *lose* on new products *before* you figure what you can make

(7) Don't waste your firm's money; spend carefully at all times

(8) Remember that an earned dollar in your pocket is worth ten dollars of a sale you haven't yet made

Pursue success and excellence and your firm will grow quickly and surely. And what will success bring you? It will bring you:

- Great wealth
- Power over others
- Prestige amongst friends
- Security from poverty

## Expand and diversify your holdings

As the prosperity of your firm grows you will be able to delegate authority to others—that is, you can get others to do your work. Then you can:

- Relax and enjoy your money
- Look around for other businesses
- Take over other firms

To take over other firms you follow the same steps you've just completed. But the situation will be somewhat different because:

- You'll have plenty of money
- You won't be rushed
- You'll have power and prestige
- People will chase after you

By following a careful program of expansion and diversification you'll be able to:

- Build from nothing to millions in a few years
- Diversify from one business to several

- Accumulate a large personal fortune
- Obtain lots of prestige
- Never have to worry about money again
- Have a happier life
- Be free of boredom

Yes, good friends, taking over several businesses can be lots of fun, and a great challenge. You'll find that your work is exciting and thrilling, instead of being boring. But what is just as important is that you'll build a fortune so fast that you won't know what to spend your money on. Truly, you won't—at least at the start! But you'll soon learn. Follow my general ideas and you can build wealth faster than you ever thought possible. Further, if you ever need a financial friend for advice, you have one in this author! Remember that.

### Use real-estate takeover techniques

Up to now we've been talking mainly about taking over industrial and service-type businesses. You can use similar techniques for "sick" real estate. By "sick" real estate I mean:

- Tax arrears sales
- Abandonment sales
- Changing-area sales
- Emergency sales

Let's take a look at each type of deal so we understand what I have in mind. Also, let me say before we start that real-estate takeovers usually require some cash—but you can borrow this—if you want to. This means your personal investment will still be zero. (Just listen to your good friend and you'll learn how to do more on less!)

### Watch for tax arrears sales

Tax arrears sales of real estate are also called *tax deficiency* sales, *tax delinquency* sales, *tax lien* sales, and by similar names. But regardless of the term used, a tax arrears sale of real estate is a sale made by a local real estate authority to recover unpaid real-estate taxes on a property. To save space we'll call any such sale a *tax sale.*

The property involved in a tax sale may be:

- Vacant land
- Developed land
- Homes—single- or multiple-dwelling
- Apartment houses
- Commercial buildings
- Industrial buildings
- Parking lots
- Supermarkets
- Any other type of real estate

A tax sale usually occurs after three or four years (or sometimes less) of non-payment of real-estate taxes. The exact time involved can vary from one locale to another. So to be sure for your area, call the tax assessor. You'll find him listed in your telephone book under . . . . . . City, or City of . . . . . or . . . . County, or County of . . . . . Ask him how long must pass before a property is sold for non-payment of taxes. He'll be glad to tell you.

### Don't miss out on big profits

Now why are tax sales important to you? Tax sales are important to BWB's because:

> At the usual tax sale, a real-estate property can be obtained for much less than its market value because tax payments for real estate are usually low, compared to the property value.

Thus, you might pick up values like these:

- A $35,000 home for $841 in back taxes
- A $100,000 apartment house for $3,622 in back taxes

(Note: *Back* taxes are *unpaid* taxes.)

Some cities and towns will sell real-estate properties at an auction, three or four times a year. At such auctions, there may be an *upset price* quoted. The upset price is the *minimum* price the city or town will accept for a property. This price is usually just a few dollars above the amount owed for back taxes.

## Have your deposit ready

At a tax sale auction or a simple tax sale held in the assessor's office, you are usually expected to deposit 20 percent of the purchase price in cash. This may be in the form of a certified check, money order, or cash. Thus, on the above two properties you'd be expected to deposit 0.20 ($841) = $168.20 on the first, and 0.20 ($3,622) = $724.40 on the second. When you make this deposit you take the first step in assuming control of the property.

While tax sales are usually made for the purpose of recovering real-estate taxes, you will also run into tax sales made to recover federal taxes of various kinds. In such sales you will usually have to submit a sealed bid for the property. In real-estate tax sales, the bidding is usually open, so you can easily see what the other person is offering. But federal tax sales, and some state tax sales, even though sealed, can be an important source of low-cost deals for you.

## Don't let tax sales trouble you

Now for a word about your private thoughts on the ethical aspects of tax sales and purchases. Both of us know that the local and national taxing authorities are entitled to their income. Hence, when you take over a property in a tax sale, you are helping either a local or national authority to collect taxes.

It's true that someone may suffer the loss of his or her property when you take it over in a tax sale. But if you didn't take over the property, someone else would. So you are doing a service to your fellow man when you take over property on which taxes are owed. Further, if you go to the trouble of paying your taxes, why shouldn't others do the same?

## Get in on abandonment sales

Abandonment sales resemble tax sales in some respects. But the reason for the sale is more than failure to pay taxes. The main reason is that the owner abandoned the property—that is, he walked away from the property and was never seen again. So the taxing authorities have an "ownerless" property on their hands. When an owner abandons a property, the usual result is that:

- Taxes are not paid
- Maintenance of the property is neglected
- Bills pile up
- Buildings may be vandalized

So an abandonment sale may give you some headaches after you take over the property. But you can get so many bargains of this kind that the money you spend fixing up a property is well invested. (And you can usually borrow whatever funds you need.)

Where are abandonment sales usually found? In the "inner city" areas of large cities. Why? Because some families are moving out of these areas as soon as they accumulate a few extra dollars. But this migration doesn't mean that the inner city is dying. There are plenty of "new poor" families who seek inner city housing which is clean, neat, and well-maintained. You can provide such housing at a profit, if you want to.

### How abandonment sales are run

Abandonment sales are held in about the same way as tax sales. Bids for local property are generally made at a public auction. If you're slightly afraid of abandonment sales, attend a few of these auctions and:

- Make notes of the price paid for each of several properties
- Note the name and address of each property
- Visit each property after the auction
- Ask yourself if you think the property is worth the price paid for it
- Estimate how much it would cost to put the property into good condition
- Estimate the income you could obtain from the property after repairs and improvements are made
- Estimate the resale value of the property

Doing this will help you lose your fear of abandonment sales. Also, you'll gain valuable *numbers experience* which will guide you when you make your first bid on an actual property. But keep one fact in mind on all tax and abandonment sales, namely:

> Never bid on a property until after you have inspected it and determined its repair cost (if any), its potential income, and its probable resale value.

### Don't overlook changing-area sales

The cities of the world are changing. In my travels throughout the world I see the same conditions everywhere, namely:

- Middle-income people are deserting the cities in droves
- Poor people are flocking into the cities
- Wealthy people are keeping their apartments, penthouses, multiplexes, and townhouses in the cities

So you find—in many cities—that the population is either very poor or very rich. This situation leads to what you might call *changing-area sales*. And what is a changing-area sale?

> A changing-area real-estate sale is a quick, reduced-price sale of valuable property caused by fear of declining property values or of unfamiliar operating problems.

You can pick up plenty of bargains in changing-area sales. But to get these bargains you must:

- Familiarize yourself with the changes taking place in your city or town
- Select those changing areas which you believe have chances of coming back
- Contact real-estate agents in the area and watch for ads for property in the area
- Negotiate a sharp deal, always remembering that the sale is being made out of fear
- Start improving the property as soon as you take title to it

Changing-area sales can make you rich in a hurry. Don't be afraid of them. Many studies of "block busting" (which is a *forced* change in an area) show that although property values may decline at first, they quickly recover. So in any changing-area buying you want to:

- Buy at the lowest price
- Hold until recovery sets in
- Sell at the highest price

## Be ready for emergency sales

Life is full of emergencies for people. You're familiar with most of these emergencies—death, high taxes, divorce, ill health, and so on. Any and all of these emergencies might lead to a sudden sale of real estate at a bargain price. If you want to hit the big money fast in real estate, using borrowed capital, then you should consider getting ready for emergency sales. Here's how.

To be ready for emergency real-estate sales you need:

- Cash on hand (*COH* I call it)
- A plan of action
- Professional help lined up
- Goals for your real estate empire

Let's take a quick look at the first of these items—COH

## Nothing beats COH

The key to success in emergency sales of real estate is ready cash, that is, Cash On Hand (COH). Why? Because:

> With cash on hand you can make a fast deposit on good
> deals, thus tying up property before others hear about it.

Remember this fact about cash for emergency real-estate sales: *The person negotiating an emergency real-estate sale often knows little about the true value of real estate.* What this person avidly seeks is:

- Immediate cash
- Quick sale
- No headaches

So if you have the cash on hand, ready to make a deposit, you're in an ideal position to satisfy all the above wants.

COH can be in several forms, such as:

- Cash in the bank
- An approved loan from a lender
- Easily used collateral (stocks, bonds)

"But I don't have any money," you say. "How can I get started?" Follow the tips on borrowing money given in *Business Capital Sources*, available for $15 from IWS Inc., P.O. Box 186, Merrick, N.Y. 11566. This book lists more than 2,000 active lenders who can help you get the money you need. You'll also find my book, *How to Borrow Your Way to Real Estate Riches*, $15 from IWS, a big help in getting money for real-estate purchases.

Other ways to improve your borrowing capacity include:

- Get a strong co-signer for loans
- Build up a good personal and company credit reputation
- Borrow collateral from friends and relatives
- Use the IWS lucky-dozen Venture Capital Search (VCS) plan

COH is vitally important to making big money in emergency real-estate sales. You *can* be ready to take on a profitable deal if you do some advance planning. Start today and you won't be left out of the good deals that regularly pop up!

### Save time when building riches

In any kind of special real-estate sale of the type we've mentioned here—tax, abandonment, changing-area, and emergency—you can save time and make money faster if you:

- Sell the property to the former owner
- Sell the property to another buyer
- Sell the property before making the final payment on it

### Let's take a look at each

Sometimes, the former owner of a property will suddenly want it back after he hears that it has been sold by the municipal authorities for tax arrears or other reasons. Now don't worry! The former owner can't get the property away from you—in most areas of the country, at least—unless he:

- Pays you what you paid for the property, plus interest on your money
- Pays you for the effort you've put into acquiring the property
- Pays you any reasonable profit you seek
- Gets you to agree to sell the property to him

Thus, there's *no* rule, in most areas, which says you *must* sell the property to him. And you can charge him a price you think the property and your efforts are worth. So you're *fully* protected against the loss of your money, time, and effort. But it's so seldom that the original owner will try to buy back the property that you'll seldom run into this situation.

Sometimes you can sell the property to another person either: (1) right *after* you make the balance of the down payment, or (2) *before* you make the balance of the down payment.

### Control lots of property for little cash

Most property auction and tax sales require a 20 percent cash down payment. Thus, you can control the property for a month or longer (depending on how long the closing takes) with only 20 percent down. And remember this is 20 percent of a much reduced price. Often, the total price of sick real estate will be only 2 percent or 3 percent of its true value on the open market.

Thus, your down payment is only $0.20 (0.03) = 0.006$, or $0.6\%$ of the actual value of the property. This means that you need only six-tenths of a cent to control $1 worth of property! That's real leverage for you.

So if you sell the property while you have only the 20 percent down payment on it, you can profit enormously. To arrange such a sales deal:

- Decide, in advance, who might be interested in the property
- Check out ways in which you might advertise the property
- Decide if there's enough of a chance of selling the property to justify spending the money for the ads

### How to make fast real estate sales

Let's say you take over an industrial property for $500 down in a distress sale. You think that industrial firms in your area might be interested in buying the property from you. Checking a local commercial and industrial review-type newspaper, you find it has a weekly circulation of 8,000 copies. Figuring an average of two readers per copy gives a total readership of 16,000. A good size ad in the paper will cost you $96. (You find this out by calling the paper's ad department.)

Now, you say, suppose that one in a hundred, or 1 percent, of the readers are prospects for buying this property. This means that 160 readers *might* buy this property. Since the ad will cost me $96, the cost per prospect is $96/160 = $0.60. This is really very cheap and the ad is certainly worth a try.

Your ad runs in a newspaper two weeks later, long before you have to put up the balance of the down payment on the property. Calls and letters come in from 35 prospects interested in the property.

You talk to several prospects and find that they're really hot on buying your property. Within a week you close a deal at a price of double your down payment. Thus, you've doubled your money in a few weeks without even having to take over the property! You've used the combined leverage of:

- Low down payment, and
- OPM—other people's money, and
- Wide advertising of your offer

Today there are few deals that can beat this approach to fast riches.

### Use the takeover road to wealth

In the above sections on business and real-estate takeovers I've stuck to the practical day-by-day, how-to-do-it aspects of these deals without too many examples of actual use. The reason I used this approach was because I felt that it was important for you to understand *what* to do, *when* to do it, and *where* to do it. Now that you understand these matters, we can look at some actual examples of putting these methods to work.

## BUSINESS TAKEOVER BUILDS TEXTILE WEALTH

Saul W. took over a sick textile mill with *no cash down,* using the *zero-cash* method you learned earlier in this chapter. He sold off some of the mill's real estate and machinery for $112,000. Two years later, after cutting the staff and expenses, his mill sold $1.6-million worth of goods for a profit of $160,000. Saul's annual salary is $80,000. Today, four years after the takeover, the mill is valued at $12-million.

## MAIL-ORDER GROWTH ZOOMS

Steve H. took over a sick mail-order business with no cash down, using the *zero-cash* technique mentioned earlier. After working out an extended debt payoff plan, Steve introduced a series of new mail-order products which he obtained free from manufacturers for mail testing purposes. Borrowing money for printing and postage, Steve turned a loser into a winner in just three months. A year after the takeover, Steve's mail-order business reached its first million in sales. "That's not bad for a beginner," Steve says, "particularly since the original company was losing money like mad and didn't cost me a penny of cash!"

## REAL ESTATE BUILDS SOLID WEALTH

Martha R. dreamed all her life of building a real-estate empire. But she never had enough money for the down payment on a suitable piece of property. When she heard of tax and similar sales, she decided to take a chance and borrow the money she needed for the down payment on her first property. Using the methods described earlier, Martha soon had $1-million worth of property under her control. And to achieve this level of wealth she never invested a cent of her own! Her only investments were time and energy.

## Borrow on your takeovers

In my work as president of a multi-million-dollar lending organization, book author, lecturer, publisher, and executive, I meet thousands of ambitious people. I try to help all these people because they come to me for help—not to see what I look like. As to the kind of help I try to give, in just one week, recently, I was able to show people how to:

- Get a $100,000 line of credit from a major bank
- Get a $400,000 compensating-balance loan from a lender
- Mortgage out (walk away with cash) on a no-cash-down real-estate deal for an apartment house
- Earn a $2,500 fee for a 1-day job as a financial broker
- Make a quick $10,000 profit in a mail-order export business

Since I work only five days a week at these various tasks, I can report only five "scores" for that week. Each score makes me happy. And judging by the reactions of these readers, each score made each of the readers ecstatically happy!

### How bankrupts are helped

But the one class of readers that gets the most bang from its scores, and from which I get the biggest thrills, is the *bankrupts.* And each year there are more personal bankruptcies in the world. People go too deeply into debt, panic, and declare personal bankruptcy.

Going bankrupt may relieve you of the obligation to pay off your debts. So it has certain attractions to some people from this standpoint. But bankruptcy ruins your credit rating. And it can take years and years (often five years or more) to re-establish your credit rating. Without a good credit rating you:

- Cannot borrow business or personal funds
- Cannot buy an auto, home, or other items on time
- Cannot be accepted as a co-signer on a loan
- Cannot wheel and deal in business matters

To put it quickly and bluntly to the bankrupt, or the potential bankrupt:

> As a bankrupt you are locked out of almost every business deal you might try to enter.

So you should make every effort possible to avoid bankruptcy. But if you've already gone bankrupt, I think I can help you.

### How to overcome bankruptcy

If you are a bankrupt, there are a number of agencies which know about you. (In using "you" in this section of this chapter, I'm not saying that *you, my reader,* are bankrupt, I'm just talking to those readers who *are* bankrupt. But bankrupt or not, read on to learn how to get rich without a credit rating, collateral, or rich relatives!)

Now the agencies which know about bankrupts are:

- Credit bureaus
- Large banks
- Large and small finance firms
- Large stores
- Auto lending agencies
- County sheriff
- City and state record offices

In other words, there aren't many people who don't know about who went bankrupt, and:

- The amount the bankrupt owes
- What his assets were
- Whom he owes money to

Thus, the bankrupt is exposed to the view of everyone who wants to know something about him. To wheel and deal in business so that he can make enough money to pay off his debts and remove the stigma of bankruptcy from his name, the bankrupt needs a "cover," "umbrella," or some other "shelter" which will:

- Serve as his credit front
- Shield him from credit spies
- Allow him to get loans of all kinds
- Permit him to earn big money

In helping bankrupts financial advisers early discovered an ideal cover for them. It can work for you whether or not you are bankrupt. Here it is.

### How to go from debts to riches

The best cover ever found for a bankrupt person is the:

- Sick business takeover, or
- Sick real-estate takeover

Why? Because:

> In sick business and real-estate takeovers, the sellers are
> usually so anxious to get out that your previous financial
> history is ignored. Thus, the business or property you
> take over becomes your bankruptcy shelter.

Once you take over the business or property, using the steps
given earlier in this book, your personal credit rating will never be
questioned. Instead, the firm's credit rating shields you from the
curious and snooping eyes of other people. Using the firm's credit
rating, even a poor one, you can:

- Borrow business funds
- Buy equipment on time (autos, boats, houses, factories)
- Enter profit-making deals
- Get financing from other businesses (this is known as interbusiness
  financing)
- Wheel and deal as you like

So you see, good friends, *as a bankrupt with a sick business,
you're much better off than a bankrupt without a business!*
Remember that I told you this:

> Even owning a sick business is better than owning no
> business at all. For a sick business can get better,
> whereas a "no" business can go nowhere!

So give some thought to taking over a sick business. It could be
your magical "out" that:

- Wipes away debts
- Gets you the possessions you need

- Allows you to repay your debts
- Puts money in your pocket
- Needs NO cash investment
- Lets you lead the *great* life to which you're entitled

## Go onto a great life

Takeovers can put you into the big chips sooner than you think. This chapter has given you many hints on exactly how to make big money in the takeover of sick companies and sick real estate. You're now ready to get started. So go out and do your thing. And good luck to you!

### SELECTED BUSINESS BROKERS HAVING NATIONWIDE CONTACTS

Affiliated Business Brokers of America, 15 Park Row, New York, N.Y., 10038. Telephone: 212-964-4222.

Associated National Business Brokers, Inc., 280 Madison Ave., New York, N.Y., 10016. Telephone: 212-889-3376.

Corporate Resources, Inc., Merger and Acquisition Specialists, 15 E. 40th Street, New York, N.Y., 10016. Telephone: 212-679-8449.

Engle, Bill Co., 80 Court St, Brooklyn, N.Y., 11201. Telephone: 212-855-0160.

Federated Business Agencies, 1790 Broadway, New York, N.Y., 10019. Telephone: 212-246-4706.

Industrial Financial Co., 60 Wall St., New York, N.Y., 10005. Telephone: 212-425-3858.

Kinsley Associates, Inc., 1440 Broadway, New York, N.Y., 10018. Telephone: 212-736-4310.

LaRue Media Brokers, Inc., 116 Central Park South, New York, N.Y., 10019. Telephone: 212-265-3430.

Madison International, Ltd., 1175 Walt Whitman Rd, Melville, N.Y., 11746. Telephone: 516-271-0479.

Merchants Business Exchange, 152 W. 42nd St., New York, N.Y., 10036. Telephone: 212-947-2134.

Merger Masters International, Ltd., 20 W. Park Ave., Long Beach, N.Y., 11561. Telephone: 516-889-1122.

National Business Exchange, 150 Broadway, New York, N.Y., 10005. Telephone: 212-267-2914.

On-Ward List Brokers, Ltd., 1 Union Square, New York, N.Y., 10003. Telephone: 212-929-0530.

Harry Spiegel, 26 Court St., Brooklyn, N.Y., 11201. Telephone: 212-875-8520.

Taurus Associates, 1775 Broadway, New York, N.Y., 10019. Telephone: 212-265-0225.

VIP Business Brokers, Inc., 133 E. Jericho Tpke., Mineola, N.Y., 11501. Telephone: 516-248-5666.

William Vandersteel, International Financing, 40 Wall St., New York, N.Y., 10005. Telephone: 212-425-5910.

World Wide Enterprises, 387 Fordham Rd., Bronx, N.Y., 10458. Telephone: 212-298-8900.

*Important Notice:*   You can also find lists of business brokers in your local area in the Yellow Pages of your phone book under the heading of "Business Brokers."

## DEALERS IN SURPLUS AND BANKRUPT
## INVENTORIES—A SELECTED LIST

AME Mills Supplies, Inc., 85 Humboldt St., Brooklyn, New York, N.Y., 11206. Telephone: 212-383-4449.

Ace Surplus Co., Inc., 8 Berry St., Brooklyn, New York, N.Y., 11211. Telephone: 212-388-9660.

Action Electronics Co., 40 Dale St., West Babylon, N.Y., 11704. Telephone: 212-895-8825.

American Surplus Trading Co., 332 Canal St., New York, N.Y., 10013. Telephone: 212-966-5650.

Amjet Aerospace, Inc., 37 W. 30th St., New York, N.Y., 10001. Telephone: 212-564-7913.

Anco Trade & Import Co., 42 Broadway, New York, N.Y., 10004. Telephone: 212-269-1527.

Arenburg Electronics Corp., 46 Fulton St., Brooklyn, N.Y., 11201. Telephone: 212-624-7038.

Atlantic & Pacific Wire & Cable Co., Inc., 137 Grand St., New York, N.Y., 10013. Telephone: 212-966-2508.

Barnett & Small, Inc., 768 E. New York Ave., Brooklyn, N.Y., 11203. Telephone: 212-473-2045.

Canal Equipment Co., Inc., 345 Canal St., New York, N.Y., 10013. Telephone: 212-966-3868.

D & D Salvage, 51 Bond St., New York, N.Y., 10012. Telephone: 212-473-2045.

D D H Inc.,3710 38th, Des Moines, Ia., 50310. Telephone: 515-279-8342.

Electromatic Equipment Co., 37 Lispenard, New York, N.Y., 10013. Telephone: 212-925-2074.

Fulton Trading Co., 245 Van Brunt, Brooklyn, N.Y., 11231. Telephone: 212-625-7301.

Industrial Materials Co., 613 2nd Ave., New York, N.Y., 10009. Telephone: 212-532-2396.

Institute of Surplus Dealers, Inc., 303 W. 42nd St., New York, N.Y., 10036. Telephone: 212-582-7390.

Luria Bros & Co., Inc., 1001 Newark Ave., Elizabeth, N.J., 07208. Telephone: 201-351-3924.

Railroad Salvage Co., 70 Britannia, Meriden, Conn., 06450. Telephone: 203-235-5721.

Surplus Associates, 75 Worth St., New York, N.Y., 10013. Telephone: 212-925-3000.

*Important Notice:*     You can also find lists of surplus and salvage dealers in your telephone book Yellow Pages.

## POINTS TO REMEMBER

- You *can* get rich in business or real estate starting with *no* money.
- Use the methods given in this chapter and you can own your own business.
- Your future may hinge on putting the zero-cash concept to work today.
- Keep trying and you're certain to move ahead.
- Remember—one of the most powerful starting methods you can use is zero-cash!

# 10

# Get <u>All</u> the Wealth
# Help You Need

Talk to self-made rich people anywhere in this world, as I have, and you'll often hear a remark that goes thus:

> "I had a lot of help on my way up and I'm very grateful to everyone who gave me a hand in building my fortune."

You can get *all* the wealth building help *you* need—and this chapter shows you exactly how. For if you were to come with me (as I wish you could) on my many trips to meet Beginning Wealth Builders (BWB's), you'd soon see that many BWB's:

- Don't know where to get money help
- Are afraid to ask wealth questions
- Waste time during interviews talking about non-business items
- Desperately need help from an experienced wealth builder or other knowledgeable person
- Need long-range plans
- Must control their time better

## Where to get business help

You can start your search for business help by taking a positive view of any sort of assistance, namely that:

> All business help ultimately leads you to greater knowledge—of yourself, your business, people in general, and

203

the world. Seek knowledge and you will soon have
power.

So you see, good friend, when you get business help you really
obtain greater know-how. And it is this know-how that allows you
to move ahead in the business that turns you on.

Your fortune-building know-how can come from many sources,
such as:

- Books (the one you are reading now)
- Periodicals (such as newspapers, magazines, a wealth newsletter, and
  so on)
- People (experienced fortune builders, consultants, businessmen)
- Government agencies, state bureaus, city officials

Let's take a look at all these wealth sources and see how they
might work for *you*. In the process, I'm sure that we'll put a lot of
extra money in *your* pocket! And friend, that's my biggest aim in
life—to make *you* rich!

## Books can be powerful

In the world of fortune building—a world I know intimately
because I've built several fortunes of my own—knowledge is
power. And books can be important sources of knowledge to *you*.

*Money books*, which is the term I use for the kind of book you
are reading at this moment, perform three major jobs for you:

(1) *Motivate you* to think, search, try, act, do—that is—urge *you*
    to take the steps that will make *you* rich.
(2) *Inform you* as to *what* you should do, *when* you should do
    it, *where* you should do what, *why* you should do what, and
    *how* you should do what.
(3) *Train you* in the elements of business, money, borrowing,
    interest, negotiations, stocks, bonds, taxes, contracts, and
    other financial transactions.

Now books, of course, will vary in the degree they motivate,
inform, and train. Those of you who've read a number of self-help
books will recall that:

- Some books are strong on motivation, weak on how-to.
- Other books are strong on the how-to aspects but are too high level for Beginning Wealth Builders (BWB's)—these books use words the BWB's can't understand.
- A few books both inform and motivate you in words you can understand. These are the kinds of books I recommend you read and study. And each book I recommend in *this* book is a useful book for *you*, which I'm sure you can understand *and* use.

Keep in mind at all times the proven fact that *good* money books can be a major factor in your life. So when you find a money book that appeals to you, keep a copy of the book near you at home and when you travel to and from work. Then you can dip into the book at odd moments to obtain incentives and information.

## Use government aids

Free books and booklets which you can get from the U.S. Government can be a big help to you. Here are a number of these free aids that were available free at the time of the writing of this book.

### FROM THE SMALL BUSINESS ADMINISTRATION

## Free business bibliographies

The following free bibliographies list many hundreds of articles, books, and other publications which may be useful to you. I think that the time you spend looking at these will be well repaid.

Handicrafts and Home Businesses, #1
Selling by Mail Order, #3
Marketing Research Procedures, #9
Retailing, #10
Statistics and Maps for National Market Analysis, #12
The Nursery Business, #14
Recordkeeping Systems—Small Store and Service T.rade, #15
Restaurants and Catering, #17

Basic Library Reference Sources, #18
Advertising—Retail Store, #20
Variety Stores, #21
Laundry and Dry Cleaning, #22
Training Retail Salespeople, #23
Food Stores, #24
Suburban Shopping Centers, #27
National Mailing-List Houses, #29
Voluntary and Cooperative Food Chains, #30
Retail Credit and Collections, #31
Drugstores, #33
Distribution Cost Analysis, #34
Hardware Retailing, #35
Jewelry Retailing, #36
Buying for Retail Stores, #37
Mobile Homes and Parks, #41
Bookstores, #42
Plumbing, Heating and Air Conditioning Job Shop, #43
Job Printing Shop, #44
Men's and Boys' Wear Stores, #45
Woodworking Shops, #46
Soft-Frozen Dessert Stands, #47
Furniture Retailing, #48
Apparel and Accessories for Women, Misses, & Children, #50
Trucking and Cartage, #51
Store Arrangement and Display, #52
Hobby Shops, #53
Interior Decorating, #54
Wholesaling, #55
Painting and Wall Decorating, #60
Sporting Goods, #62
Photographic Dealers and Studios, #64
Real Estate Business, #65
Motels, #66
Manufacturers' Sales Representative, #67
Discount Retailing, #68
Machine Shop—Job Type, #69
Automatic Merchandising, #70
Sales Management for Manufacturers, #71
Personnel Management, #72
Retail Merchandising and Promotion, #73
Retail Florist, #74

Inventory Management, #75
Pet Shops, #76

See Chapter 1 for directions for ordering these publications.

Most Government publications, magazine articles, and technical books are *factually* very useful. But if money books—that is, books which combine both facts *and* motivation—interest you, then I recommend that you seek out these kinds of books, too.

One of the best lists of money books that I know of is the one which is part of the IWS *"Starting Millionaire" Program.* This list gives you the author, title, publisher, price, and a short description of more than 5,000 money books. Having this up-to-date list on hand can be a big help.

Another good list of money books is in the Prentice-Hall general catalog. Look under the various self-help headings that might interest you, such as:

- Advertising
- Business Management
- Hobbies
- Inspirational
- Taxation
- Self-Improvement

I'm sure you'll find a number of useful money titles listed in this helpful catalog.

### Read every day of the year

Business is always changing. How? In many ways. Almost every year there are changes in:

- Business laws
- Taxes on business
- Government regulations
- State requirements
- Business personnel

To keep up with these changes, you should read a good general newspaper, business newsletter, and business magazine. Many large cities have good general newspapers which cover both the usual news and business items. My favorite daily newspaper is the *New York Times* because it gives excellent coverage of all news.

In the area of business newspapers I think that the *Wall Street Journal* and the *Financial Times* (London, England) are excellent for the *experienced* wealth builder.

In the area of business newsletters I think that none can beat the monthly *International Wealth Success* which regularly gives both beginning and experienced wealth builders:

- Thousands of easy-money lending sources
- Hundreds of money-loaded capital sources
- Numerous sources of 100 percent financing
- Zero cash real-estate and business deals
- Unusual borrowing ideas
- Unique profit sources
- Many finder-fee offerings
- Business consulting opportunities
- Hundreds of other valuable leads
- Monthly Ty Hicks column

No other newsletter that I know of gives these kinds of leads at the nominal price of $24 per year. To subscribe to this excellent newsletter, send $24 to IWS Inc., P.O. Box 186, Merrick, N.Y. 11566.

Other helpful newsletters include the following which serve one or more business areas:

- *Business Week Letter*
- The *Kiplinger Tax Letter*
- *Acquisition Newsletter*
- *Foreign Projects Newsletter*
- *Inside Industry*
- The *Kiplinger Washington Letter*

In business today there is no substitute for reliable information. So, if you want to build your riches faster, spend some time reading good up-to-date periodicals every day. Useful magazines which give you a broader picture of the business situation include: *Business Week, Fortune, Forbes, Barron's* and *Dun's Review.* You can find copies of these magazines in any large city library.

## Get help from people in business

Many business people are happy to help beginners interested in getting started. To get help from such people you must:

- Learn to listen
- Be ready to soak up facts
- Try using other people's methods
- Have a young, student-like outlook
- Be ready to follow orders

In my travels throughout the world, I've been amazed at how readily many businessmen share their know-how. Many of these people had to work for years to obtain the skills and information they have. Yet they are often willing to share their skills with you if you just show the slightest interest in *their* business!

## One way to learn about real estate

Larry L. used the *interest* technique to learn all he could about Florida rental real estate. Living in the north, Larry didn't have much time to spend in Florida to learn what he wanted to know. So he:

(1) Got the name of several rental property owners from real estate agents he called in Florida.
(2) Wrote the owners, telling them when he would be in Florida, and asking for an appointment.
(3) Visited several owners, and *listened* while they talked about their problems.

In less than a week, Larry came, saw, learned, and bought— using OPM (other people's money). Since building wealth is 99 percent in your head, here's a quick rundown of what Larry learned that helped him pick profitable property in less than a week. In Florida:

- Yearly rentals are the key to a steady income.
- You have an unlimited labor supply from the thousands of retirees.

- Ten or more units in a building reduce your vacancy risk.
- Waterfront property costs more but earns you a higher profit.

Today Larry has a whole string of profitable rental buildings in sunny Florida. And he is busily expanding his holdings. The total cost of his quick education in Florida real estate? Less than $500!

## Where to meet business people

You *can* meet knowledgeable business people in many different ways, including:

- Phoning local experts and making a date to visit them
- Writing to experts and asking for an appointment

When you're not in the same city or town, you're probably better off writing to the expert. Your letter can be short or long—both work. But be your letter long or short, don't start it by telling the expert how:

- Wrong he is
- How poor you are
- What troubles you've had

Try, if you can, to begin with a complimentary comment about his work, reputation, or other aspects of his career.

## Accentuate the positive

To understand how the business expert thinks, put yourself in his position for a moment. You're asking him to give you useful information which:

- Uses up his time
- Takes his energy
- Does not give him any income

To make him do what *you* want him to do—give you information—you have to start on a positive note.

Sometimes a reader who calls or writes to me (and thousands do) starts with a long, sad tale of a series of business and personal failures. Such an approach really turns me off because I immediately begin to feel a wave of negative emotion passing through me. The result is that I have trouble warming up to the reader even though I want to help him.

So, to get a better start with any business advisor (and particularly me), accentuate the positive by:

- Highlighting your skills
- Focusing on your ambition
- Turning failures into learning
- Seeing the bright future you have

Friend, I've traveled many a mile in this great world of ours while rising from near-poverty to riches of all kinds—family, friends, accomplishment, recognition, fun, and money. And I am so convinced that the positive-thinking, ambitious BWB can make it big that I refuse to talk to the "Wailing Nellies" of this world. Why should I, or any other business advisor, waste his time on the negative Nellies when there's so much we can do for, and with, the positive thinkers and doers?

So, accentuate the positive in all dealings with business advisors. You make life easier for each of you. And further, you help yourself more because you give the advisor more time to help *you.* And that, after all, is why you went to him in the first place!

## Get lists of business advisors

You can regularly get the names and addresses of business advisors in the pages of the monthly newsletter, *International Wealth Success.* Many of these advisors list in their ads the types of businesses for which they consult.

The *Yellow Pages* of any large city telephone directory list business consultants under various headings, such as *Management Consultants, Business Consultants,* and the like. A phone call to the consultant's office will quickly tell you if the daily fees, or job charges, are low enough for your business budget.

The Small Business Administration maintains a listing of retired businessmen interested in consulting (at no cost other than their daily expenses) for small- and medium-size businesses. You can obtain the names of these consultants by calling any office of SBA. You'll find the SBA under the *U.S. Government* listing in your phone book. Chapter 1 of this book contains a list of SBA office addresses.

Finally, your author is willing to consult with you—free of charge—on your business questions. A letter to me, in care of my publisher, is all you need to get started. But please remember that the busy schedule I follow may not meet with *your* need to see me tomorrow or the next day because I may be in Europe, or elsewhere. So please—for *your* sake—have a little patience. Thanks!

## How to work with an advisor

You can get excellent results from many business advisors if you know how to work with them. Here are a few profit-laden hints for you that will help you build great riches sooner.

(1) Never pay an advisor for a preliminary survey of your business—he should be ready to do this free.
(2) Ask the advisor to tell you about other, similar businesses he has helped in the past.
(3) Have your advisor show you figures on the actual results he achieved at other businesses.
(4) Check with his other clients to learn what kinds of results they obtained from the advisor you are considering.
(5) Never sign a contract, or agree to pay a fee until you are sure you want to deal with a specific advisor, based on your checking him out.
(6) To get the best results from an advisor, listen to him, hear what he says you should do.
(7) Make the final decisions yourself—after you've studied your advisor's ideas. Don't blindly follow what someone else says. Analyze, compare, think, then decide for yourself!

## Help is where you find it

Life is often strange. You might go to a top-level (and price) consultant for advice and come away with only modest help. In contrast, you can be on a plane, train, bus, or an elevator, after seeing your top-level consultant, and one chance overheard remark in a nearby conversation can open an entire world of profit to you.

I've often wondered if the chance remark that so many BWB's mention having overheard would have meant as much to them if they had *not* gone to the consultant or advisor. I guess this question can never be answered because you can't go back and re-live the situation.

After years of making money for myself and many others in many different businesses, my advice to *you* and *your* advisor is:

(1) Read as many good books on the specifics of fortune building as you can. (Many millions of readers, I say *very* humbly, have found my various money books—listed at the start of this book—of some help in building their fortune; you also might discover the same.)

(2) Keep up to date with regular publications directed at helping *you* build wealth quickly. The best such publication I know of is the monthly newsletter *International Wealth Success.* You might find that this idea-laden newsletter can be a big help to you, too. And running free ads in it as a subscriber may get you the business money you need.

(3) Read a good local newspaper *every* day. Keep up with the business news in *your* area.

(4) Take a course in business. Pick your course in such a way that it leads you to immediate career actions *and* results. Typical courses you might wish to consider are those given in local schools and colleges, correspondence courses and the IWS self-study courses, namely the *Financial Broker Program;* the *"Starting Millionaire" Program;* the *Mail-Order Riches Program;* the *Franchise Riches Program;* and the *Zero-Cash Easy-Money Success Technique Program.* These excellent self-study courses show you exactly how to get started in your own wealth-building activities. Priced at $99.50 each, they are well worth the price. The first two courses include four handsome diploma-like framable certificates which you can hang on your office wall.

(5) Keep a friendly outlook on all business people. Your best advisor is often a person in the same business you are considering.

You are now ready to start using a business advisor. No matter whom you select, I hope you find the hints in this chapter helpful *and* profitable!

## POINTS TO REMEMBER

- Many self-made successful fortune builders are ready to help you with free advice.
- You can get plenty of business help from books, periodicals, people, and government.
- Read something about business *every* day of the year.
- Business newsletters and magazines can be a big help to you.
- Consultants can guide you to greater success.
- Try to see the positive side of every situation.
- Business help is wherever you find it; you'll find help if you look for it!

# 11

# Build Great Riches
# in Your Own Home

Most of us are "homebodies"—that is, we love our homes. True, most of us like to travel now and then. But no place in the world is as dear to us as the place we call home.

As boy and man I've traveled the world on ship, plane, train, bus, and private auto. Yet no city has ever looked so beautiful to me as my hometown—New York—on a beautiful spring day when seen from the deck of a ship in the lower bay, or from the first-class seat of a sleek jet swooping down over the Atlantic Ocean onto JFK International Airport. And I've always believed— and told people—"If a guy or gal can make it in his hometown, he can make it anywhere in the world."

Today I'd expand that statement to: "If you can make a fortune anywhere, you can make it in your own home." Let me show you exactly how.

## You can get rich in your own home

I've made close to a million dollars in my own home. If I could do this, I'm sure *you* can do the same, or better, because when I started building my home fortune there were no:

- Books telling how
- Publications for home wealth builders
- Vast opportunities such as those that exist today

Making money in your own home can be a pure delight because you:

- Avoid surly bosses
- Have a steady income
- Won't be fired or laid off
- Don't have to take orders
- Can plan and control your fortune

Plenty of people throughout the world run a business in their home. And some of these people earn one million dollars, or more, in their home business within just a few years. I'm so certain you can do the same that I'm about to show you exactly how to start and operate *your* own home business.

### How to start your own home business

There are certain businesses you can run better in your own home than you can anywhere else. These businesses include:

- Mail order
- Import-export
- Real estate
- Franchise sales
- Financial broker
- Product or process licensing

Each of these businesses is considered in this book. Right now, let's see how you can get started in your own home business.

To start a business at home, take these five lucky steps:

(1) Pick the business having the best profit potential for *you*.
(2) Check out the possibility of running this business from your home.
(3) Form your business by (a) registering it with the County Clerk in your area, (b) setting up a partnership, or (c) establishing a corporation. For (a) and (b) you may be able to get along without an attorney, but for (c) you should definitely have an attorney.
(4) Have a letterhead and envelopes printed, using your business name and your home address. (Or, if you prefer, use a post

office box number for your business address. Many of the
world's largest corporations operate from a post office box.
Having a post office box saves you from being called on by
salesmen, customers, and others you may, or may not, want
to see.)

(5) Get a business telephone listing. (You can use your home
phone, if you wish.) But if you'd prefer not to have calls,
don't use a business phone listing. Plenty of home businesses
get along without any telephone number for their business.

## Get your business rolling

It shouldn't take you more than two days to take care of the
five steps above. With these steps taken, you are ready to get
your business rolling—that is, bringing in money that you can
deposit in *your* bank.

To get your business rolling you must:

(1) Let people know you're in business
(2) Convince people of the worth of your service, product, or
business
(3) Start selling your product or service

Since you will probably have more ambition than money at the
start, I suggest that you use your ambition in place of money to:

(a) Publicize your business
(b) Get free distribution of ads
(c) Have people endorse your offers

To get income-producing mileage from your ambition:

(1) Send out product and service releases for free publication in
newspapers and magazines.
(2) Carry advertising material with you at all times and pass it
out free to everyone you meet who is a potential customer.
(3) Use every free ad source that is open to you. For instance,
the *International Wealth Success* newsletter is reported to
give excellent results to their one-year or longer subscribers

who can run *free* ads in the newsletter as often as they want, when space is available.

(4) Use your local newspaper, shopper's guide, and other news media to get whatever coverage you can for your product or service.

(5) If you make, import, or export a product of any kind, send $25 to IWS Inc., P.O. Box 186, Merrick, NY 11566, for their *Product/Service Publicity Kit.* This big kit contains all the forms, names, addresses, and other data you need to get a good start on obtaining free publicity and ads for your home products and services.

Use a results-directed approach in all your advertising and promotion activities. By a results-directed approach I mean:

(a) Naming what you want to achieve (such as publicity in a certain magazine).

(b) Deciding how you'll achieve the objective you listed in item (a).

(c) Taking action, and pushing ahead until you reach your goal.

### Be ready for loneliness

Working in your own home business has many advantages and is lots of fun, particularly when the money starts to roll in. But, like every other business, a home business has certain drawbacks. One of the biggest drawbacks I can think of is the loneliness you may meet.

When you work alone you're more likely to be lonely because you:

• Can't be certain of results
• Have no one to share your problems
• May be confined to one small area

Recognizing that a problem exists is the first step in solving it. If you feel that loneliness will be part of your home business problems, then take steps to reduce the impact of the problem by:

• Getting out of the house at regular intervals to breathe some fresh air.
• Going someplace *useful* such as your local public library where you may learn something.

- Meeting *interesting* people, and *helpful* ones. Remember that interesting people may not always be helpful people. So try to meet both types!
- Having a hobby which is different from your business can help you overcome loneliness and can give variety to your life.

## Be your own expert

In your own home business you'll often need the advice of an expert to solve a problem in:

- Advertising
- Management
- Public relations
- Production
- Some other special field

As a beginner, you may think that you know very little and that only an expert can help you. This is certainly true, of course, in legal, medical, scientific, engineering, and similar matters. But in the more routine areas of business, take my advice and:

> Be your own expert—after you study suitable books and courses. You'll learn more and earn more if you take this advice.

To help you become an expert on various business subjects, I've listed some helpful books and courses for you at the end of this book. You might want to check them out in your local library and bookstore.

## Build home wealth fast

I know plenty of people who have a home business. Some make *big* money ($50,000 per year, and up) fast. Others just scrape by. From my observations, the kinds of so-called home businesses that will put only a few bucks in your pocket after a lot of work are those that take you out of your home, such as:

- Newspaper delivery
- Rug cleaning

- Reweaving of garments
- Home furniture repairs
- Pizza delivery
- Lawn and garden care
- Oil burner overhaul
- Office and home cleaning

Now please note the character of each of these businesses. Your income is restricted by your:

- Available time
- Physical energy
- Local area size
- Selection of the type of business

Thus, in these and similar businesses, your activities limit your income! Yet few home wealth builders know this when they first start out. To help you pick a home business which can make you at least one million dollars, here's a list of a few you might want to consider. Each can easily make you a million in a short time. These businesses are:

- Mail order product sales
- Book publishing
- Magazine or newsletter publishing
- Export-import
- Product licensing
- Real estate rental
- Stock and commodity market investment

Few of these businesses restrict your profit potential by imposing severe physical or mental strain on you. Many of these businesses are discussed in various chapters in *this* book, and in several of my other money books. The main fact to keep in mind about any home business is:

> Be careful not to pick a business which is self-limiting with respect to profits, unless you have set a low profit goal for yourself. Aim for the stars and you have a much greater chance of reaching them!

## Avoid the problem businesses

In every business, including *every* home business, you have problems. These problems lead to what I call the *aggravation factor* in a business. And if you're like me, I think you'll want to keep *your* aggravation factor as low as possible in *your* home business.

Why is a low aggravation factor important? Because:

> The more you can concentrate on making money in your home business, the larger your income can become. But aggravation from business problems cuts your income and annoys you personally.

Home businesses which have high potential aggravation—that is, they may drive you up a tree with problems—include the sale of:

- Foods or medicine
- Fragile products of any kind
- Extremely heavy or large items

Also, any activity which borders on the questionable, such as the following, can lead to problems:

- Home-brew "cures" of diseases
- Non-professional dental remedies
- Debt consolidation
- Unordered merchandise
- Fund raising for dubious causes
- Children's day-care centers
- Old folks' homes

After years in business, my personal conclusion is that you sleep better and rest easier if you are 100 percent honest in *all* your business dealings. You may need a little longer to hit the big money when you do it honestly. But at least you do it with peace of mind! And every big success I've ever known has told me that his experience verifies this thought. Further, I'm convinced that it's easier to hit the big money honestly than dishonestly!

### Keep pushing your home business

At home you'll often be lonely, and you may also have the feeling of being:

- Unloved
- Unwanted
- Unappreciated
- Misunderstood
- Deserted

With all this negative feeling around, some home business people neglect their work. This is really sad because:

> Neglect of your business brings on more problems, leading to greater loneliness and trouble.

The best way to fight your loneliness is to *work!* Why? Because:

- Work is *constructive*
- Work builds your *fortune*
- Work *combats* loneliness
- Work *creates*—continuously
- Work *fights* destructive forces

So, please take my advice—if you want to make big money in your own home business in your spare time. Make work your hobby, instead of making problems your hobby! With solid, useful work as your main activity, you are sure to make it big in your own home business.

### How others hit the big money

In my role as author, business adviser, businessman, worldwide lecturer, and friend of the needy, I meet thousands of new people every year. A number of these new friends run their own home businesses. I'd like to tell you about a few of these people to show you how you can hit the big money in your own home business.

## FRANCHISE MILLIONS FROM HOME

John T. wanted to franchise what he thought was a great idea—having clothing custom-made overseas for people in the United States, Britain, and Europe. His clothes would be custom-made in Asian countries from measurements taken by a franchisee (the person who buys a franchise) in the developed country—such as the U.S., Britain, or France. Or the franchisee could hire people in his area to take the measurements. Everyone could work in, and from, his own home.

John was lost as to how to sell his franchise until he came across the IWS *Franchise Riches Program.* Costing $99.50, this big *Program* tells you exactly how to get started in franchising your ideas so that people *pay you* to use your ideas, instead of *you* paying others for their ideas.

Using the *Program* as a guide, John decided to franchise distributors for his product—made-to-measure clothing—for a fee of $800. This is really an ideal franchise because:

- The fee to franchisees is low
- No other big investment is needed
- It's really a low-cost "paper" business
- Products are lightweight, air shippable

Working from his home, John T. sold $1-million worth of franchises in 18 months. Today, he continues to expand his home business to take it nationwide, then worldwide.

## HOME WOODWORKING PROFITS

Monty K. loves to work with rich, beautiful woods. From these woods he carefully carves decorative figures of all kinds—fish, animals, people, flowers. Monty started carving when he and his wife lived in a city apartment. Today, since buying his own home, Monty works in his basement workshop which is fully equipped with all the tools he needs.

Several years after he started carving in wood, Monty showed one of his carvings to a gift-shop owner. The owner was entranced with the carving. "I could sell that the first day I had it," he said enthusiastically. "It's yours," Monty replied immediately.

Since that day Monty's carvings have been selling in an increasing number of stores. Using the Ty Hicks approach, Monty has:

- Priced his carvings high
- Sought fewer sales at higher prices

- Kept promoting his carvings
- Recognized the gross-dollar method

In the *gross-dollar method* you say to yourself, as Monty did for his products, which are carvings:

(1): 10 products sold at $1,000 each = $10,000 income
(2): 1000 products sold at $10 each = $10,000 income

Which would I prefer to have (1) or (2)? Monty, using my approach to business and life, chose (1). And the delightful result was, and is, that people are happy to pay Monty's prices.

Today, Monty has a booming carvings business. Many of his items are specially ordered, meaning that Monty is paid even higher prices per item carved. And by standardizing his "special" items, Monty has been able to get young woodworkers to do much of the routine work so that he can concentrate on the fine finish needed.

## COSTUME JEWELRY AT HOME

Dr. Floyd K. is a medical specialist during the day. But at night he turns to another specialty at home—costume jewelry.

Starting as a hobby, Dr. Floyd's jewelry soon became a business. Since he enjoys his jewelry work, Dr. Floyd both designs and makes the pieces. Typical prices for his home-workshop produced costume items range from $100 to $1,500.

While Dr. Floyd's medical practice is growing, so too is his jewelry business. He has no intention of leaving medicine or jewelry. And Dr. Floyd's home business income will soon rival his medical income— which isn't small!

## REAL ESTATE FROM AN APARTMENT

Can a beginner really hit the big money in real estate working from his own home? He sure can, as David T. is demonstrating every day of the week.

David heard through the monthly newsletter, *International Wealth Success,* about my ideas on *zero-cash real estate.* This is real estate that you take over with *NO CASH DOWN* of any kind. Since David T. had no capital to start his own business, the zero-cash approach really intrigued him.

Using the methods recommended by smart real-estate operators, David was able to take over some 300 rental apartments with NO cash down. The average rental of each apartment is a little over $100 per month and most real-estate operators use a "talking" vacancy rate of 5%. Thus, David's monthly income is: 0.95 (300 units) ($100 per month per unit) = $28,500. And his yearly income is (12 months) ($28,500 per month) = $342,000.

Of course, there are many major expenses such as mortgage payments, taxes, maintenance, labor, and so forth. But even so, using an average net income of 20 percent of the gross rentals, David's income from his zero-cash investment is 0.20 ($342,000) = $68,400. Not bad for a beginner working from his own home without an office, big staff, or expensive equipment!

"But is his work easy," you ask. No; his work *isn't* easy. David has to supervise rent collections, maintenance, apartment rentals, and other details. But no matter how hard he works, David keeps reminding himself that spare-time home operation of zero-cash real estate is probably the only way he could hit the big money fast. And you can do the same—starting today.

## MAIL ORDER HOME RICHES

Millions of people dream of making a fortune in home mail order. Thousands buy, every year, special catalogs at reduced prices from drop-ship firms. Then they mail these catalogs to rented lists, often working from the kitchen table at home. Some people make home money this way, and some don't.

A better way (in my opinion) to make big money in home mail order is that used by Bert and Rhoda K. (called B & R from now on). B & R started with the idea that they wanted to:

- Market unusual products
- Use special mailing lists or ads
- Charge high prices
- Control their business future

With these ideas as their basic guide, B & R started to look for unusual products. After searching for months, they found what they wanted on a farm in a little mountain town in Tennessee. Their product? Parts of ancient automobiles, such as headlights, horns, steering wheels, foot pedals, windshields, control handles, running boards, spoked wheels, radiator caps, radiator emblems, and all the rest. Their gold mine was a deserted auto junkyard containing some 200 rusted and forgotten wrecks.

B & R set about salvaging as much of each car as they could. Where possible, they removed the parts using simple hand tools. Where hand tools would not work, B & R used portable blow torches. The farmer in whose field the ancient autos rested was delighted to have the eyesores removed from his land free of charge.

With 100 parts salvaged, B & R sat down and prepared a simple listing of their products thus:

| | |
|---|---:|
| 1921 Stutz headlamp | $ 55.00 |
| 1921 Stutz radiator | 170.00 |
| 1930 Ford Model T windshield | 87.50 |

With their list finished (it ran three typed pages), B & R prepared simple classified ads for the shelter (home) and auto hobbyist magazines.

The ads read as follows:

---

*Shelter Magazines*
Decorate your home with beautiful
parts from old autos. Send for
complete list of parts and prices.
B & R, P.O. Box 1, Anytown.

---

*Auto Magazines*
Decorate your den, garage, or car
with parts of antique autos. Send
for complete list of parts and prices.
B & R, P.O. Box 1, Anytown.

---

Each ad contained the firm name and address in its last line (where a dummy address is shown above). Running the ads for just one month produced an avalanche of inquiries. And some 23 percent of those who asked for the price list bought one or more items from B & R. The names of these customers became the core of the B & R mailing list.

Bert and Rhoda's real breakthrough came when Rhoda decided to use some of the antique car parts in products she designed for homes, offices, and new cars. These unique products—such as a coffee table made from an old spoked wheel—sold out instantly at high prices. Within a few months the B & R mail-order and direct-mail business was booming at record levels. Today B & R is a leading, growing, quality mail-order house which Bert and Rhoda still run from their home.

## Home riches can be yours

You *can* make a fortune in your own home. Plenty of people have done it. And many more *are* doing it today.

The beauty of building a fortune in your own home is that you get away from all barriers of:

- Age
- Sex
- Color
- Experience
- Appearance
- Education

More non-high-school and non-college graduates have made it big in home businesses than in almost all other kinds of businesses.

I'm so sure that *you* can make it big in *your* home business that I write a monthly column for the newsletter *International Wealth Success* in which I discuss many aspects of business, including those run in your own home. You might find the column interesting, and helpful.

Why not try your own home business, using the hints in this any my many other money books? You have nothing to lose but the money you don't earn!

### POINTS TO REMEMBER

- You *can* get rich in your own home business.
- Making money in your own home business can be delightful because it rids you of many problems.
- Getting started in your own home business costs you almost nothing.
- Seek every free ad and publicity outlet you can find.
- Try being your own expert in the non-professional areas of your home business.
- Be careful *not* to pick a business which is self-limiting in the profit area.
- Avoid problem businesses if you want peace of mind.

# 12

# Make the Real Estate Boom
# Build Your Millions

Real estate is always with us—from the moment we're born until the day they tuck us away in a six-foot plot. In between these two moments, every human being occupies varying amounts of real estate every day and night of his life.

## See real estate as it really is

Today real estate—land and structures—is so valuable that:

- Railroads are selling the air rights above their tracks
- Property owners are selling rights to land covered by water
- Oil companies rarely sell gas stations—instead they lease them, thereby retaining ownership of the land
- Old, unused buildings are being repaired and restored for sale at high prices

And there are many other examples, some of which you can see in your own neighborhood. "Why is this happening in real estate?" you ask. Because:

> Real estate is a limited-supply commodity. As the number of people in the world increases, so does the demand for real estate.

228

If you travel as I do, you'll see that real estate is in great demand everywhere. No matter what form of government or political system people live under, every man and woman ultimately seeks his own little piece of land. This desire is basic in every human being everywhere. So when you build your fortune in real estate you deal with important human needs. This is why I want you to consider real estate as a way to your great fortune.

## Nine other reasons for you

While the basic drive for property is universal, it is *not* the only reason for the popularity of real estate. Other factors leading to a wider demand for real estate include:

- More leisure—the short work week is getting shorter
- Greater wealth—people have more money to spend on property
- Stronger desire for the "good" life
- Wider recognition of the investment potential of real estate

I'm sure that once you see real estate as it really is, that is:

- Potentially highly profitable
- Loaded with lasting values
- Filled with tax-saving possibilities
- Income producing every moment of the year
- Highly leveraged, giving you big profits on other people's money

you will want to check to see if you should be making money in real estate.

## How you can make money on OPM

OPM—other people's money—is one of the most powerful tools available in the world today. Why? Because with OPM you can:

> Put borrowed money to work for yourself to earn a profit for yourself and the lender while providing essential services—such as housing for others.

You, by contributing your know-how, energy, and ambition, make the other person's money do more for the entire world— including yourself. And note this fact now—*the OPM you use may come from:*

- A bank
- A mortgage lender
- The federal government
- A state government
- The general public
- An industrial development commission
- A private lender
- A city government
- A venture-capital firm
- An insurance company
- A corporate lender
- A partnership, either limited or general
- A savings-and-loan association
- A building-and-loan association

Thus, you have at least 14 *common* sources of OPM to finance your real estate deals. (If you can list more, great.) This is more sources of capital than any other type of business is eligible to tap. Hence, you stand a greater chance of getting rich quickly in real estate on OPM than in almost any other business. Let's see how you can put OPM to work, here and now, in real-estate deals that can make you a millionaire in just a few years.

### Watch OPM make you rich

Let's say you want to buy a well-kept income-producing residential property having a total price of $100,000. To find out how much you can borrow on this property you refer to an extremely useful book, *How to Borrow Your Way to Real Estate Riches,* available for $15 from IWS Inc., P.O. Box 186, Merrick, N.Y. 11566. This book quickly shows you how you can borrow up to $50-million and up to 100 percent of the purchase price of a residential property using an FHA-guaranteed mortgage with a payoff of 40 years.

Let's say that you borrow 80 percent of the total price. Now 80 percent of $100,000 is 0.80 ($100,000) = $80,000. To complete this deal using OPM, you need $100,000 - $80,000 = $20,000 more. "Where," you ask, "can I get the extra $20,000?"

There are plenty of places, such as:

- Banks specializing in real estate
- Second-mortgage lenders
- Mortgage brokers
- Insurance companies
- Corporate lenders
- Venture-capital firms

You'll find thousands of such lenders listed in *Business Capital Sources*, available at the same price from the same source as the book mentioned above.

So you borrow the $20,000 on a second-mortgage basis for five years. (Most second-mortgage loans are limited by the lender to no more than seven years.)

As you receive income from the property, you pay off your second mortgage *and* your expenses. If you figured the deal carefully, you should be able to walk away with a nice profit, say $1,000, every month.

Soon you take over several other properties, using the first property as part collateral for the second, and so on. Before you know what has happened, you're sitting back enjoying a lucrative, trouble-free income of $10,000 per month, each and every month, from your properties.

### Know real estate ins and outs

To see how the real estate you buy using OPM can make you rich, glance at the typical profit and loss form, Figure 12-1, for a property. At the top you have your annual income from rents, say $70,000.

Next you have your expenses. Included in expenses are mortgage payments, real-estate taxes, maintenance, light and heat, wages, insurance, and any other costs you must pay to have the property run for you. Let's say all these expenses total $50,000. Then your annual profit, which I like to call MIF (money in *your* fist or "cash throw") is $70,000 - $50,000 = $20,000. That's a neat return from a property for which you didn't put up a dime of your own money!

Now some "profit and loss" forms will show the mortgage payments as "profit." Don't be fooled by this. Remember the Hicks fortune builders real estate riches rule:

> Never buy any real estate which does not give you money in fist or cash throw each month and each year.

### TYPICAL INCOME-PROPERTY ANNUAL PROFIT

|  |  |  |  |
|---|---|---:|---:|
| Income from rents |  |  | $70,000 |
| Expenses: |  |  |  |
|  | Mortgage payments | $30,000 |  |
|  | Taxes | 5,000 |  |
|  | Maintenance and repairs | 2,000 |  |
|  | Labor | 6,000 |  |
|  | Light and heat | 3,000 |  |
|  | Miscellaneous | 4,000 |  |
|  | Total expenses |  | $50,000 |
| Net profit |  |  | $20,000 |

**Figure 12-1**

### Search for your profits

You must recognize that you go into the real-estate business for one purpose—to earn a profit from, and on, the properties you buy. Thus, every step you take should be aimed at your profit purposes. Now here are a number—26 to be exact—of valuable ins and outs of real estate which can put money into your pocket in the form of profit dollars. I call these pointers my:

### ABC's of Real-Estate Riches

ALWAYS plan to raise the rents on your property to keep up with inflation.

BUILD your income on a solid base of know-how obtained from study of good business and real-estate books and courses.

CONSERVE your capital—buy and operate your real estate on borrowed money.

DON'T give up your search for good real estate; keep looking every day.

EXPECT a few problems in real estate; then you'll be ready for them.

FIND your fortune in real estate by looking, looking, looking for the best property locations.

GOOD real estate *is* available to those who seek it.

HIRE poor people to run your buildings; you'll help others and save money.

INCREASE your real estate income by regularly raising rents.

JOIN a real-estate association in your area—you'll learn from it.

KNOWLEDGE is power, particularly in real estate.

LET others run your properties while you sit back and develop new profit ideas.

MAKE real-estate profits your goal and you'll never have to worry about money.

NEVER give up your search for real-estate profits.

OWN real estate and you'll get richer sooner and with less risk.

PLAN each real-estate deal carefully and you'll make money from it.

QUESTION every price that is quoted to you in real estate and many people will reduce their "asking" amount.

REPAY mortgages as slowly as possible—this will put more profit in your pocket.

SELL your real estate as soon as it starts losing money.

TREAT your tenants well but charge the highest rent legally allowed.

UNDERESTIMATE profits and *overestimate* expenses before you buy any real estate.

VERIFY income and expense statements by checking the property's income-tax returns.

WHEEL and deal on the price and terms before you buy any piece of real estate.

"X-RAY" every real-estate deal *before* you go into it.

YELL and shout for lower prices and higher rents in all your real estate deals and holdings.

ZEAL pays off in real-estate deals, so build your enthusiasm for profits.

## Wheel and deal for your real estate

*Never* pay the asking price for real estate. Why? Because the asking price in *every* real-estate deal *always* contains a "pack" or

### Table 1: Typical "Pack" Percentages for Real Estate*

| Price of Property (Land and Building(s)) | Typical "Pack" Percentage |
|---|---|
| $ 5,000 | 10% |
| 7,500 | 10 |
| 10,000 | 10 |
| 12,500 | 10 |
| 15,000 | 10 |
| 17,500 | 10 |
| 20,000 | 9 |
| 25,000 | 9 |
| 35,000 | 8 |
| 50,000 | 7 |
| 60,000 | 7 |
| 80,000 | 6 |
| 100,000 | 5 |
| 150,000 | 5 |
| 200,000 | 4 |
| 250,000 | 4 |
| 300,000 | 3 |
| 350,000 | 3 |
| 400,000 | 3 |
| 500,000 | 2 |

*Note:* The percentage shown can vary from one area to another.

"cushion" which the seller puts in, hoping that some fool *might* pay the asking price. If you pay the asking price without trying to do some wheeling and dealing (which is really fun for most people), the property may cost you 5 percent to 10 percent more than it should. And that 5 to 10 percent is enough to cover the closing costs on many deals. (Closing costs usually include your lawyer's fee, insurance payment adjustments for the property, tax adjustments, and similar items.) Now let's see how the "pack" works.

Table 1 shows typical pack percentages you can expect for many buildings in various price ranges. While these pack percentages are the typical ones I've observed, you may find that in your area they are somewhat different. If this is so, just enter the numbers for your area in a similar table.

Note in Table 1 that the pack percentage is higher at the lower prices of real estate and lower at the higher prices of real estate. The reason for this is that the dollars available for the "pack" are fewer at the lower prices; hence the percentage is higher so any potential deal will be more attractive. Thus, on a $10,000 property, the pack might be 10 percent, or $1,000. This means you'd expect to pay $10,000 - $1,000 = $9,000 for the property. But on a $100,000 property, a pack of 10 percent would be $10,000, which is probably too high. A $5,000, or so, pack (which is 5 percent) is much more likely. You'd then pay $95,000 for the property.

### Six secrets for building fast real estate wealth

You can get richer, faster, and easier in real estate if you know:

- Secret shortcuts you can take
- Financing aids to get your money
- Tips on running your properties

Real estate is one business in which you can get capital by borrowing even though you have little or no credit or collateral. That's why you can build a fortune faster in real estate than in almost any other business—if you know the secrets of how to run your business efficiently. Here are my real-estate secrets. This is the first time they've appeared in print anywhere.

## REAL-ESTATE SECRETS THAT CAN MAKE YOU RICH

(1) BORROW YOUR WAY TO REAL-ESTATE WEALTH. *Never* put up a cent on real estate if you can borrow the money.

(2) MORTGAGE YOUR WAY TO RICHES. Mortgage every penny you can on your real estate.

(3) GET AS LONG A MORTGAGE AS YOU CAN. The longer the payout period, the lower your annual payment and the more cash in your pocket. Also, the higher your deduction for interest on your income-tax return.

(4) FIGHT FOR THE LOWEST INTEREST RATE POSSIBLE. The lower your interest rate, the smaller your annual payment. A rough rule of thumb is that your payment, for principal only, goes up about $4 per year per $1,000 financed, for each 1/2 percentage increase in interest.

(5) BUILD YOUR REAL ESTATE FORTUNE ON THE INCREASE IN VALUE OF YOUR PROPERTY. Make each property improve your financial statement by showing its larger value on the statement when you borrow to buy the next property.

(6) BUY YOUR FIRST PROPERTY USING BORROWED MONEY. Then finance *every* other property using other people's money.

## Build your real-estate wealth with paper

Some BWB's (Beginning Wealth Builders) want to build their real-estate wealth by constructing new buildings. Although this is an admirable dream, there are easier ways for you to start making *your* fortune in real estate. The ways I like to use need only paper, such as:

- Loan applications
- Mortgages for land and buildings

- Deeds for property
- Promissory notes for money
- Compensating balances for loans
- Time deposits for banks
- Construction loans
- "Standby" loans
- Long-term commitment loans
- Letters of credit
- Interim financing
- Sale-leaseback deals
- 100 percent financing of property
- FHA-insured loans

Can you really build *your* real-estate fortune with paper? You certainly can! Here's a typical, easy-to-use technique that puts 100 percent financing to work for you.

### How to get 100 percent financing for your deals

To get 100 percent financing for a real-estate deal you need the 12 magic Hicks ingredients for fast wealth. These are:

(1) Locate a suitable property—such as vacant land or land with one or more commercial or industrial buildings on it.
(2) For vacant land, prepare a neat presentation package (a concise, typed description) showing what commercial or industrial buildings you might construct on the property. (For buildings already built, prepare a neat plan showing how you could improve them for existing and future tenants.)
(3) Prepare a listing of the rents you'd charge for each building in your project. (To learn about going rents in your area, check with local real estate dealers.)
(4) Send copies of your presentation package to local real estate agents, large and small newspapers, nearby large firms, and people who might want to rent space in your proposed project.
(5) Ask for long-term leases of your buildings. (This means a ten-year, or longer, lease.)
(6) If you get one or more inquiries from profitable firms

concerning long-term leases, ask the owner of the property if he'd hold it for you on an exclusive basis for ten days, or longer. (To do this, ask him to send you a signed letter saying that he's holding the property for you on an exclusive basis for ten days, 20 days, or 30 days—the longer the better for you. An anxious seller will usually write you such a letter at no cost because he hopes to make the sale.)

(7) Once you have this "exclusive" letter, and the inquiries from interested tenants, visit one or more banks or mortgage lenders. Show them your data on the property and ask them how much you could borrow using the property *and* leases as security. (You'll find that most banks and mortgage lenders welcome such deals and will usually lend *all* the money—that is 100 percent—you need to buy and develop the property.)

(8) Having a promise of the money you need will work miracles with your prospective tenants because they know the property is nearing the point where it can be taken over. Write your prospective tenants and tell them that you want a letter from them saying they will rent space for ten years or more, when the project is completed.

(9) Using these letters, go back to your lender and apply for a property purchase and/or construction loan.

(10) With the money in hand, buy the property and have the construction begun, if building is necessary.

(11) If you need extra money during the construction of your project, go back to the lender and ask for an interim financing loan.

(12) With the project finished, apply to your present lender for long-term financing (up to 40 years). Use this money to pay off your earlier loans. Then watch the money roll in as your real estate fortune increases day by day.

## Be nimble, be quick

The 12-step magic real-estate riches plan for 100 percent financing of your fortune building you just read can work miracles in your life. But to use this plan you must be nimble and quick. Why?

Because 100 percent financing of any business deal is a skillful blending of

- Men and women
- Money
- Materials, and
- Motivated minds.

To beat the competition, you have to work sure-footedly and quickly. Only then can you make the prize of 100 percent financing yours. Let me show you how four other Beginning Wealth Builders (BWB's) went from near-poverty to great riches in real estate using 100 percent financing.

## BECOME A PARKING-LOT TYCOON

The simplest real estate operation (other than vacant land) is a parking lot. Ben Z. sensed this before he decided to become a parking-lot millionaire. Why is the parking lot so simple? Because all you need is a small portable shed for the attendant—nothing else, not even paving, lights, fences, or other equipment.

And how did Ben Z. get 100 percent financing for his parking lots? Very easily—by starting with a $5,000 business loan from his bank. With this $5,000 in hand, Ben *rented* a local parking lot in a large city for several weeks. Using part of the $200,000 annual income of the rented parking lot as *his* income (based on his lease of the lot which had an extension clause), Ben borrowed $100,000 from a private lender. This money was enough for a down payment on his leased lot, plus two others.

Thus, in a matter of four weeks Ben went from a nominal income of $8,000 a year to a gross income of some $300,000 per year. This is what I call *"instant wealth."* I like it because you use OPM. (NOTE THE FINANCING TECHNIQUE USED HERE: Use the income from rented or leased property as the basis of a large loan.)

## TAKE OVER SHOPPING CENTERS

Laura K. loves to meet people. Her second love is shopping. Those two hobbies made a good combination for the shopping-center magnate which Laura became in just a few months using 100 percent financing.

To take over her first shopping center, Laura got a second mortgage loan from a second mortgage lender. The true annual interest rate was 18 percent but Laura figured this was cheap, compared with:

- No second mortgage
- No interest cost
- No property ownership
- No real-estate income

Her first shopping center (whose earnings paid off the second mortgage in two years) gives Laura an annual income of $75,000. Subsequent purchases of other shopping centers, using the first shopping center as collateral, have raised her annual income to $260,000. Not bad, when it was all done on OPM! (NOTE THE FINANCING TECHNIQUE USED HERE: Use of multiple mortgages to produce enough cash to purchase a property with 100 percent financing.)

## BUY PROPERTY USING THE SELLER'S MONEY

You can buy *some* properties using a P.M. mortgage. The P.M. stands for Purchase Money. A purchase-money mortgage is a loan the *seller* of a property makes to you, the *buyer*, on the closing of a deal.

Robert C. used a P.M. mortgage to buy a $100,000 commercial building. His bank financed 70 percent, or $70,000, and the seller gave Robert a seven-year $30,000 purchase-money mortgage to close the deal. Using these two sources of funds, Robert took over the building without putting up a penny of his own.

*You* can use a P.M. mortgage in almost every real-estate deal where the seller is willing to issue one. In effect, your P.M. mortgage is a "second" mortgage on the property. Most P.M. mortgages are short-term, running three to seven years. (NOTE THE FINANCING TECHNIQUE USED HERE: Buy property using the seller's money to finance part of the deal.)

## MORTGAGE OUT AT MORE THAN 100%

*Mortgaging out* means getting more cash from a mortgage (or mortgages) than you need to buy a property. Thus, Ken L. took over a $250,000 income-producing property this way, with the following financing:

| | | |
|---|---|---|
| Total price of property | | $250,000 |
| First mortgage | $200,000 | |
| Second mortgage | 30,000 | |
| P.M. mortgage | 50,000 | |
| Total loans | | 280,000 |
| Cash received by buyer | | $ 30,000 |

From this cash, Ken had to deduct "closing costs" of about $10,000, leaving him a net of $20,000. The big and important points here are that Ken:

(1) Invested NONE of his own money to get started
(2) Took over a profitable income property by investing only time and knowledge
(3) Walked away with money in his pocket after giving himself a big monthly income
(4) Took over a property which will almost surely rise in value as time passes
(5) Started himself on the way to his real estate fortune
(6) Got started on *zero-cash*

The result of all Ken's effort is visible to Ken today and will continue that way for as long as he carefully supervises his business. (NOTE THE FINANCING TECHNIQUE USED HERE: Obtaining mortgages of a larger amount than needed to take over a property.)


## Never stop looking

Yes, you can make *your* fortune in real estate. To get started, all you need do is look around yourself and see the real-estate boom at work. This boom will be visible to you on every populated street in the world.

To help you get started, I'm including in the appendix a list of helpful real-estate books. You might want to read one or more of these books to widen your knowledge of real estate. Put your brain to work and you'll soon have other people working for you in one or more successful real-estate projects!


### POINTS TO REMEMBER

- Real estate *can* make *you* rich—quickly and easily.
- Real estate is a borrowed-money business—you can use OPM when you need it.
- Paper is a big part of every real-estate deal.
- You can wheel and deal in every real-estate purchase or sale.
- Real estate is the *one* business where you can be paid for buying an income.

# 13

# Become an "Instant Millionaire" Today

You can work for just two people in this world: (1) yourself, and (2) another person. Many people shun working for themselves because they believe that in holding a good job they have:

- Future security
- A dependable pay check
- Promotion potential
- Sympathy from their boss
- Many fringe benefits

On some jobs you do have all these advantages, plus others. But on plenty of jobs you have

- Little or no security
- Undependable pay
- Small promotion potential
- No sympathy from the boss

For these reasons, I often urge my readers to consider the joys, and pains, of working for themselves.

**Make it big on your own**

Working for someone else can be great, *if* your boss is kind and understanding. But working for someone else can also be boring, dull, worrisome, and uncreative if your job doesn't interest you or your boss lacks understanding.

Now I'm *not* against working for someone else for a salary. That's the way most BWB's get their start in their fortune-building program. But I do say this:

> Your chances of hitting the big money while working for someone else are nearly nil. When you work for yourself your chances are much, much greater.

Making it big on your own can be one of the most rewarding experiences of your life—and possibly the biggest thrill of your life. And making it big in your own business can put more money into your pocket than nearly any job you might hold. Let's see if I can prove to *you* that these claims are true for you, your family, and your friends.

### Put speed into your wealth search

"Everything in life takes time," a man once said. This is true. But some people in this world take less time to do things than other people do. So I'm suggesting that it might pay you to do things faster in your search for wealth. This doesn't mean that you'll be constantly rushed; it just means that you'll do things more surely, more serenely, and with greater faith in your successful building of a millionaire's fortune.

"But how can I do things faster?" you ask. "Almost everything takes *some* time."

That's true. But you can get things done sooner, and more efficiently, if you:

- Concentrate on one deal at a time
- Keep several deals going at once
- Work with efficient people
- Insist on, and obtain, deadlines
- Set, and keep, time goals for yourself
- Pick fast-growth business deals
- Borrow as much money as you can
- Keep working day and night

Using the e techniques, you should be able to earn one million dollars in three years, or a little sooner. This is what I call becoming an "instant millionaire." If you can build a million-dollar income faster than in about three years, great! I'd like to meet you and learn from you because my methods are the three-year type.

### Pick your fast-growth business

By now I hope you're partially, or fully, convinced that if you're ever going to hit the really big money, you'll have to do it in your own business. Truly, good friend, there is very little chance for you to do it any other way. With this fact in mind, let's pick *your* million-dollar business.

To earn the big-money income that you'd like to have, I recommend that:

> You try to stay close to the money aspects of every business deal. And if you can get into the money business itself, you may find it very interesting—and profitable.

Now what do we mean by staying close to the money aspects of every business deal? Just this.

> Instead of spending all your time on production, design, selling, or other operations, spend more time on financial planning, new business deals, and other ventures.

A well-known self-made millionaire recently remarked: "I never do anything myself which I can pay others to do." You can pay others to

- Build
- Sell
- Design
- Plan

- Operate
- Type
- Draw
- And so forth

But when it comes to staying close to the money, only *you* can do that. Why? Because:

> You are much more interested in your money than anyone else; hence, you can take much better care of your money.

Now let's see how you can stay closer to the money in every business deal.

## Keep close to the money

Staying closer to the money in every business deal can make you richer faster because you:

- Negotiate all loans
- Sign all contracts
- Take care of your bank accounts
- Approve all spending
- Keep a daily eye on income
- Make *all* final decisions
- Know exactly where your business is
- Keep up to date on tax costs

In staying close to your money, you avoid routine, boring, low-level work that you can pay others to do. Of course, at the start of your business you may have to do these chores because you can't afford to pay others to do them. But as soon as you can spare enough money to pay for help, you will hire people to do the "dog work" of your business.

While others take care of day-to-day chores in your business, you can give more of your time to:

- Planning future moves
- Selling new items or ideas
- Finding ways to cut costs
- Seeking new customers

Let me give you two examples of successful BWB's who use my ways to build great wealth every year of their lives.

## Sell your way to wealth

Don P. is an exercise enthusiast—he loves outdoor and indoor sports because they keep him trim and lean. While thinking of how he might convert this interest into a business, Don found that most people would prefer to have their muscles exercised for them by someone else, as is done in a massage salon. So Don decided to study the business potential of various types of massage salons and parlors.

In a week Don found that these businesses:

- Are highly profitable
- Have only two major costs—rent and wages
- Are simple to operate
- Have a year-round, steady income
- Can use part-time help
- Cost little to start

With this information in hand, Don decided to look for a suitable going massage business. Two days after making this decision, Don found a three-workroom massage salon for $10,000. Not having this much cash on hand, Don applied for a $5,000 business loan at his local bank. His loan was approved the next day. Then Don called the business owner and offered him $5,000 cash with an other $3,000 to be paid over a three-year period using promissory notes. The owner agreed to this offer. Thus, Don was able to buy this business at $2,000 less than the asking price by offering a large cash down payment.

By the middle of the next week, Don owned the business. Thus, in two and a half weeks Don went from the situation of being an employee to that of a business owner. Six months after first becoming interested in massage parlors, Don owned a total of eight. His weekly income from these eight massage centers is $2,000. With a growing clientele of both men and women, Don looks forward to a net income of $1-million a year for himself in less than two years after he started.

"So what did Don *really* do?" you ask. Here's what he did. He:

- Built a BIG income *fast* (just three weeks to get started).
- Used OPM (other people's money) to get started.
- Expanded quickly to raise his income.

So you see, it *can* be done. You *can* become an "instant millionaire"—if you take the right steps—starting here and now! But first let's see how another BWB hit it big.

### Advertise your way to riches

Clem R. wanted to go into mail order because he:

• Enjoyed working at home
• Disliked bossy bosses
• Wanted his own business
• Sensed that mail order was profitable

Yet Clem didn't want to sell rubber stamps, matchbooks, printing, or similar items by mail. What Clem wanted to do was to sell an important product (at least important in his opinion) to people who would benefit from the product. So Clem started to look for this product.

Two days later, Clem met an ex-convict who had dropped out of high school while engaged in his life of crime. During his criminal career this man was arrested, tried, convicted, and sentenced to prison. While in prison, he decided to try to finish his high school education.

In the prison library, the convict found a set of four books specially designed to help people pass the exam for the high school equivalency diploma. He studied these programmed books and within two months passed the exam with an extremely high mark.

Later, to his delight, the convict learned that almost every college in the country—including many ivy-league schools like Harvard and Princeton—accepts the high-school equivalency diploma as qualification for entrance. In fact, it was the convict's acceptance by an outstanding college that got Clem thinking about the four books in the course. If the convict could generate enough enthusiasm and interest in the course to pass the exam with high marks while in prison, why couldn't the man in the street? Clem decided to try to find the answer, using one of the best-known techniques for promoting courses of all kinds—classified ads.

### Know your business numbers

Clem went to his local library and sat down with a copy of *Standard Rate and Data—Consumer Magazines.* Thinking about the nearly million high-school dropouts per year, Clem asked himself: "What magazines might they read?" Here's a partial list of the magazines which Clem chose for his classified ads for the course:

*Popular Mechanics*
*Popular Science*
*Mechanix Illustrated*

Adding up the total readership of the magazines he chose, Clem found that 50 million people per month would have a chance to see his ad. The total cost to run a 28-word classified ad in each magazine would be $2,200 per month. Clem assembled this information in about one hour.

Now Clem had to do some deep analysis. If 50 million people saw his ad every month, how many might write for more information? (This is known as *generating inquiries*.) And of the number who wrote, how many might buy his course at $49.50? (This is called *converting to a sale*.)

Clem estimated that one of every 25,000 readers *might* ask for more information about the course each month. This meant that Clem would get 50,000,000/25,000 = 2,000 inquiries each month.

Clem also estimated that he could "convert"—that is sell—20 percent of the inquiries using a series of four letters. This would give him 0.20 (2,000) = 400 sales per month, or an income of 400 ($49.50) = $19,800 per month. From this gross income, Clem had to deduct these actual and estimated costs:

## MONTHLY COSTS

| | |
|---|---|
| Advertising | $ 2,200 |
| Materials for course @ $14 ea. | |
|     for 400 sets | 5,600 |
| Postage for inquiries and courses | 2,800 |
| Labor | 2,000 |
| Overhead (rent, electricity, etc.) | 200 |
| Total monthly costs | $12,800 |

Since Clem's total monthly income from the course sale is $19,800, his monthly profit, before his salary is: $19,800—

12,800 = $7,000. On an annual basis this is: 12 (7,000) = $84,000 per year.

### Take action–don't delay

As soon as Clem analyzed these figures–which took him about two hours–he decided to move ahead. But instead of rushing out to spend $2,200 for his first month's advertising, Clem decided to run a few inexpensive test ads. Since he was in a hurry, Clem ran them in three weekly magazines because he didn't have to wait as long to get results as with a monthly magazine.

Using the hard-sell headline–*High-School Drop Outs: Get Your H.S. Diploma and Be Accepted By the College of Your Choice*–Clem had an enormous response to his ads. Based on this response and his actual conversion rate (22 percent), Clem went to a local bank and borrowed $5,000 to finance more advertising. Within three months after starting to think about this business, Clem was grossing $20,000 per month, and growing rapidly. This is what I call becoming an "instant millionaire" which means:

> *Fast* study of deals
> *Quick* go, no-go decisions
> *Speedy* tests where needed
> *Rapid* borrowing of needed funds
> *Fast* growth of the business

Using the "instant-millionaire" approach, you should be able to:

- Build a $100,000 income in one year
- Triple this the second year to $300,000
- Become a millionaire in your third year

But even if you do not hit it exactly as I think you will, you haven't lost anything. Why? Because if you do, let's say, only half as well as I think you can do, you'll still be ahead of the people who never try!

Useful government publications you might want to check in your fast wealth-building activities are:

## FREE FROM SBA

### Business bibliographies

Selling by Mail Order, #3
National Mailing-List Houses, #29
Drugstores, #33
Hardware Retailing, #35
Jewelry Retailing, #36
Mobile Homes and Parks, #41
Bookstores, #42
Job Printing Shop, #44
Sporting Goods, #62
Real Estate Business, #65
Motels, #66
Automatic Merchandising, #70
Pet Shops, #76

See Chapter 1 for ordering directions.

And if you want extra help in trying to become an "instant millionaire," I suggest you buy the *"Starting Millionaire" Fortune Builders Program* from IWS INC., P.O. Box 186, Merrick, NY 11566. Costing $99.50, this hard-hitting, personalized program shows you how to hit it big—fast—in real estate, mail order, export-import, buying a going business, and in many other similar fast-growth activities. When considering buying this great program, just remember this:

> You CAN get rich faster and sooner than you think.
> Plenty of people have, and you will too—if you choose carefully and work hard.

### Push ahead to greatness

Believe in yourself, what you're doing, and your eventual success. With such an outlook you can't go wrong. Further, you'll soon find that others also believe in you and your work. And if you seek business activities which help others you'll get a warm glow within yourself as you watch others benefit from your work while your fortune grows. Truly, you'll be happy in friends, funds, fellowship, and fun! Could anyone ask for more in life?

## POINTS TO REMEMBER

- Some jobs offer much less security than people realize.
- You *can* make it big in your own business.
- You can speed your wealth building, if you try.
- Pick a fast-growth business.
- Pay others to do as much as possible for you.
- Keep close to the money while you sell your way to wealth!
- Seek the fast way to your fortune, fun, friends, and financial security.

# 14

# Build Millions from Pennies
# in Your Own Business

One of the easiest and quickest ways to build millions from pennies is to franchise your business ideas. If you think of a franchise as a business deal in which *you* pay, then I have a suprise for you!

Why? Because the way I see franchises is that *people pay you!* That's right—I want you to be the franchisor—that is the person who grants (or sells) the franchise and gets *paid* for it. That's a lot better than being a *franchisee*—that is the person who has to pay for *your* franchise.

### Build millions from pennies

You can easily start your own franchise business and begin to:

- Collect fees from franchisees
- Have people work for you at no cost
- Share in your franchisees' profits
- Build a great credit rating
- Expand without a sizable investment

To start your own profitable franchise operation you do, however, need something. Just what do you need? You need:

- An idea that will make money for others
- Special information, techniques, or facilities to put your idea to work

- A willingness to teach others
- A desire to help others while helping yourself

In working with numerous Beginning Wealth Builders (BWB's) who are taking the easy, franchise route to wealth, I notice that some are a trifle naive when they first think of going into franchising. Thus, many of these BWB's think they can sell almost any idea (which usually means *no* idea) to a franchise buyer. This just isn't so!

You can easily build millions from pennies in franchising. But to do so you must have something to offer the buying public. Without a valid franchise-type offer you can run into problems in franchising. This chapter shows you how to get rich in franchising, starting with a salable offer and a few pennies of your own, or of borrowed money.

## Advantages of franchising for you

To get a picture of the advantages of franchising for you, let's take a close look at the cash flow, before expenses, available to *you* from typical franchising activities. We'll assume that you sell 100 franchises at prices ranging from $500 to $50,000 each. These, as you probably know, are typical price ranges for franchises of various types. Only a few franchises that I know of cost more than $50,000. Now here's *your* cash flow, before expenses:

### TYPICAL FRANCHISE CASH FLOW

| Franchise Price, $ | Number of Franchise Sold | Cash Flow to You, $ |
|---|---|---|
| 500 | 100 | $    50,000 |
| 1,000 | 100 | 100,000 |
| 2,000 | 100 | 200,000 |
| 3,000 | 100 | 300,000 |
| 5,000 | 100 | 500,000 |
| 7,500 | 100 | 750,000 |
| 10,000 | 100 | 1,000,000 |
| 15,000 | 100 | 1,500,000 |
| 20,000 | 100 | 2,000,000 |
| 25,000 | 100 | 2,500,000 |
| 30,000 | 100 | 3,000,000 |
| 35,000 | 100 | 3,500,000 |
| 40,000 | 100 | 4,000,000 |
| 50,000 | 100 | 5,000,000 |

Your selling and other expenses for a franchise deal will run between 20 percent and 50 percent of your cash flow. So you can easily see that a franchise can be a pleasantly profitable deal for you. And if you follow my recommendations, it will be *highly* profitable! How do I know? Because I'm a franchise wheeler-dealer from way back!

## What you can franchise

You can franchise almost any business, provided you have some specialized know-how about it. But *you must have this know-how*. Without know-how which can help others, you are lost.

Now here's a partial list of business deals you can franchise. This list will, I hope, suggest other deals which *you* can consider franchising at a high profit to your franchisees and yourself:

Fast food (hamburgers, waffles, pancakes, and the like)
Special education (electronics, computers, or travel agent)
Business services (bookkeeping, tax returns, inventory control, etc.)
Protection services (guards, alarms, animals, etc.)
Automotive care (mufflers, engines, speedometers, brakes)
Boating services (boat rental, marina operation, boat sales, fuel)
Cleaning services (coin laundries, coin dry cleaning, office cleaning, floor polishing)
Personnel hiring (temporary help, permanent help, etc.)
Lodging (motels, hotels, campsites, etc.)
Real-estate services (brokerage, leasing, repairs, etc.)
Personal services (shoe repairs, hair styling, individual grooming, etc.)
Health services (karate and judo schools, vitamin sales, swimming lessons, body massage)

You can probably name other businesses which you can franchise. Great! The more ideas you can generate, the better for you. You'll find that your ideas will often flow faster and more easily if you use government publications or books written to help the small businessman.

Useful government publications you might want to check for help in generating ideas for your franchise wealth building are:

### FREE FROM THE SMALL BUSINESS ADMINISTRATION

## Free management aids:

How to Analyze Your Own Business, #46
Steps in Incorporating a Business, #111
Publicize Your Company by Sharing Information, #165
Financial Audits: A Tool for Better Management, #176
Effective Industrial Advertising, #178
Breaking the Barriers to Business Planning, #179
Expanding Sales Through Franchising, #182
Matching the Applicant to the Job, #185
Checklist for Developing a Training Program, #186
Marketing Planning Guidelines, #194
Is the Independent Sales Agent for You? #200

## Free marketers' aids

Checklist for Going Into Business, #71
Checklist for Successful Retail Ads, #96
Finding and Hiring the Right Employees, #106
Are You Ready for Franchising? #115
Training the Technical Serviceman, #117
Knowing Your Image, #124
Profit by Your Wholesalers' Services, #140

See Chapter 1 for ordering directions for any of these aids.

If you want to study the type, price, and other features of typical current franchise offers, I suggest that you buy the very useful *Franchise Riches Program* from IWS Inc., P.O. Box 186, Merrick, N.Y. 11566, for $99.50. This helpful big course lists (among its many other outstanding features) some 300 franchise firms and tells you the:

- Service or item franchised
- Number of franchises sold
- Number of states in which franchises were sold

- Price of a franchise of each company
- Training offered or required
- Services offered a franchisee

### Learn franchise facts from others

Franchising is a competitive business. To compete, you must have an attractive "package" to offer. And, if you're just getting started, you have to learn what other successful franchisors are offering. The best way to learn what the competition offers is to:

> Study a series of ads for franchises as if you are thinking
> of investing in each franchise yourself. Make a list of
> what features in the ads appeal to you.

Listing what others do which appeals to you puts you in a smart-money position because you'll be ready to become an *innovative thinker*—if you want to do so. By that I mean you can *improve on or expand the ideas suggested by others after they've proven that the ideas are profitably marketable.*

By learning what's making the other fellow a million dollars or more, and improving on or expanding his idea, you save yourself an enormous amount of money which you might spend for market research. Instead, you allow him to spend the money for researching the market. Once you see he's doing well, you improve on his idea and offer a *better* franchise. Such innovation is regularly done and can pay off handsomely.

### What's a successful franchise idea?

A successful franchise idea, in general, is a business concept which:

(1) Others can use easily, quickly.
(2) Doesn't require extensive training.
(3) Has a profitable market.
(4) Won't take too much of your time.
(5) Is simple, easy, and workable.
(6) Will earn you a good profit.

Thus, a franchise to build machines to put men on the moon or on distant planets probably wouldn't work because:

(1) Others *couldn't* use the franchise easily, quickly.
(2) Extensive training *is* required.
(3) The market is extremely *small* and is probably unprofitable.
(4) You'd have to devote your *life* to the franchise.
(5) The idea is *complex*, difficult to manage.
(6) Your profit potential is *questionable.*

So take my advice when planning a franchise product. That is:

> Pick a franchise product or concept that has a large general market (such as fast food or autos) or has a specialized professional (doctors, dentists) or business (bookkeeping, taxes) market.

To pick such a franchise, study what others are doing, using the *Franchise Riches Program* mentioned before.

### Nine magic steps to getting started in franchising

Here are my nine magic steps to help get *you* started in profitable franchising within a few days after you begin. Try these nine lucky steps—they won't cost you more than a few pennies.

(1) Pick your franchise idea. Use the hints given above and the *Franchise Riches Program.*
(2) Choose a suitable selling price for your franchise. Use the *Franchise Success Guide* book in the above Program and the following list as a guide:

| TYPE OF TRAINING AND SERVICE YOU OFFER YOUR FRANCHISEES | SUGGESTED FRANCHISE PRICE |
|---|---|
| Basic instruction and guide booklets; product discounts; little or no formal training in your business facility | Up to $1,000 |
| Some formal training in your facility; moderate super- | |

| | |
|---|---|
| vision of the business for up to one year; product formulas or preparation data | Up to $5,000 |
| Special formal training; careful supervision of the business; consulting help; special equipment designs or exclusive sales offers | $10,000 to $50,000 |

(Note: You can also use a graduated scale of prices, depending on the size of the territory your franchisee is assigned; the larger his sales area, the higher his franchise price.)

(3) Select how you'll publicize your franchise. You can get pages and pages of free publicity for your franchise offering if you prepare and send out your news story to magazines and newspapers. You can also, of course, advertise your franchise offer. But I suggest that you delay spending money on advertising until *after* you've sold your first franchise. Instead, I suggest that you seek, and obtain, free publicity in all the magazines and newspapers that might be read by people interested in the type of franchise you are offering. Later in this chapter, you'll find a list of a number of magazines you might wish to consider using to publicize *your* franchise.

(4) Decide how, and where, you'll train franchisees. I recommend that you train your franchisees by mail, using manuals and guides you prepare. Mail training may not always be possible, however. If face-to-face training is necessary, I suggest that *you* go to the franchisee—if you have the time and energy. Where the training must be done in your shop or place of business, have the franchisee come to you—at *his* expense. Study the *Franchise Success Guide* book mentioned earlier to learn about the training other franchisors offer.

(5) Decide what other services you'll offer your franchisee. These services might include:

- Site study and selection
- Help in store design and planning
- Keeping the books of the business
- Accounting and legal advice
- Consulting on special problems
- Market research studies
- Financial guidance and help

Read, if you have time, the government publications listed earlier and the *Franchise Success Guide* book to learn which services are offered by various franchisors. Then pattern your offer along competitive lines.

(6) Develop a unique aspect for your franchise. Anyone can copy an existing hamburger or ice cream franchise. But the man or woman who does this has little chance of hitting the BIG MONEY unless he can make his product *different from the rest in an appealing way.* And you—and only *you*—have the ability to find, and bring out, the unique aspects of *your* franchise offer. So study, in the government publications and the *Franchise Success Guide,* what other franchisors offer. Use the information you gather as your springboard to a unique franchise which will sell and sell, throughout the world. In fact, I recommend that you *not* "go to market" with your franchise offer until *after* you've worked out the unique aspect of *your* offer.

(7) Prepare a preliminary advertising plan. I recommend that you *not* advertise until after you sell, and receive the money for, at least one franchise. But this hint doesn't mean that you should delay planning your advertising. Often the planning on paper of your advertising, will:

- Help you see more sales points
- Show you competitive advantages
- Enable you to pick a good trade name

So sketch out some typical ads you might run. Then write some good, strong selling copy to promote your franchise sales. You'll have fun and I guarantee that you'll learn something about:

- Youself
- Your offer
- The franchise business
- What points sell

The IWS *Franchise Riches Program* mentioned earlier shows examples of many actual franchise ads which you may find interesting and useful. In this *Program* you'll also find a Special Report on making big money in franchising written by the author of this book.

(8) Study the franchise business carefully. You may benefit from a complete study of the franchise business, including such items as:

- Franchise agreements
- Capital sources for you and your buyers
- Typical ads run by franchisors
- Offering "packages" of 300 franchisors
- Steps for selling your franchise
- Many other valuable tips

Such a study will put money into your pocket if you're interested in taking the franchise route to great wealth.

(9) Try out your franchise idea on others. Talk to prospective businessmen. Describe your franchise to them. Ask them the following questions and keep a record of the answers:

(a) Does this franchise idea appeal to *you*?
(b) How much would *you* pay for this franchise?
(c) Would *you* buy this franchise instead of another?
(d) How could this franchise offer be *improved*?
(e) Does this idea really have a *future*?

Study the results you obtain from these questions. Don't limit the circle of people you ask. Go beyond your friends to strangers in your town and in neighboring towns and cities. Try to get as wide a cross section of people as you can to answer your questions.

If the responses you get to the five questions above are, in general, favorable, then you know you're on to a salable franchise. You're now ready to sell it to your public.

### Now sell hard and truthfully

Two important facts you should know about selling *any* franchise are:

(1) You *must* sell hard at the start.
(2) You *must* be truthful at all times.

These two facts go together because sometimes when a person has to sell hard, the sales pitch departs from the complete truth.

Yet in franchising we must always be truthful with our prospective franchisees if we are to be successful. So be truthful at all times. Truly, you are better off losing a prospect than misleading him into your deal.

How can you sell your franchise? There are plenty of ways, including:

(1) Contact friends and relatives
(2) Send out news releases to magazines and newspapers. (See news releases of franchises in magazines for the usual wording.)
(3) Send information on your franchise to the Small Business Administration, Washington, D.C. 20402, and Department of Commerce, Washington, D.C. 20402. In each case, send your news release to the Executive Director.
(4) Advertise your franchise wherever you can get *free* ad space. Thus, the IWS newsletter *International Wealth Success* runs free ads for its subscribers. Other free ads might be run in your local town paper, fraternity magazines, business association journals, and similar publications.
(5) Tell everyone you meet about your new franchise offering and the many advantages which it promises.

A movie star is sometimes quoted as having said: "There's no such thing as *bad* publicity!" While I'm not sure that I agree 100 percent with this idea, it is nearly correct, in my opinion. So if you want to cash in on your franchise, work at getting as much *free* publicity and advertising as you can. Just keep this fact in mind:

> To hit the big money in franchising of your ideas, you must sell hard and truthfully.

### Help your franchisee and yourself to big profits

A franchisee (a person who *buys* a franchise from *you*) is usually:

- Not your employee
- Not your partner

- In need of help from you
- Ambitious and hard-working
- *Expecting* help from you

Recognize here and now that regardless of the type of franchise you sell, you'll have to help your franchisees. This help can vary from some general advice you might offer on the telephone to full-scale training for several weeks in your own shop, plus continuing advice and consultation. For your first franchise, I suggest that, if possible, you choose one which:

- Requires the least training
- Takes little consulting effort
- Can be handled by written instructions

Now, how can *you* help your franchisee? There are several ways you should consider using, *after* he has paid his franchise fee. Each of these methods will work for you. Here they are:

(1) Meet your franchisee in person—face to face. Talk to him. Tell him:

- How much he can earn
- How soon he can earn this amount
- What work he'll have to do
- Where his best chances are

(2) Train your franchisee, if necessary, by:

- Showing him *what* to do
- Telling him *how* to do it
- Answering his questions *quickly*
- Being patient at *all* times

(3) Keep in touch with each franchisee by:

- Letter or memo
- Telephone calls
- On-site visits
- Offering special tours, trips, and the like as prizes for your successful franchisees

(4) Offer special assistance to any franchisee who is having business problems. Be sure that you:

- Don't leave him on his own
- Listen to his problems
- Offer help whenever you can
- Keep encouraging him

Help your franchisee and you help yourself. The success record of new business is very low—fully 80 percent of new enterprises fail in their first two years. Franchised businesses have a much better record—only 3 percent fail during their first two years!

Why is the success record of franchises so high? Because franchisors *help* their franchisees. This puts money into both pockets, as it will in yours, if you take action to help every one of your franchisees. Don't neglect *big* profit opportunities when they're right in your own backyard!

## Expand your business and your income

Your first franchise sale will bring you more joy than profit. But your second, third, fourth, and so on, franchise sales will bring you more profit than joy! And, after all, profit is the name of the franchise "game" we play.

You can't make money selling only one franchisee a franchise. To make money in franchising you have to expand and sell a number of franchises. The exact number of franchises you have to sell to make money depends on the:

- Franchise price you charge
- Amount of training you give
- Materials you supply franchisees
- Profit sharing arrangement you have
- Type and cost of advertising you run

Few franchisors make big money by selling only five franchises. Between five and ten sales, most franchisors begin to show a nice profit. Beyond ten sales the profit picture usually becomes extremely interesting.

Now how can you expand *your* franchise business and income? There are a number of profitable ways you can use, including:

- Advertising your franchise offer
- Having successful franchisees find prospective franchise buyers for you
- Tailoring your franchise offer to local area conditions
- Developing related franchise or product offers
- Diversifying into other businesses

Let's take a quick look at each of these methods of expanding your business and income

## ADVERTISING PAYS OFF

Publicity can help you get free notices in print when you first start your franchise. But for the sustained expansion and growth of your business you have to keep your message in front of the public. And the best way to do this is by regular advertising in suitable media—magazines, newspapers, or television, and radio.

Where are franchise offers usually advertised? Much depends on the type of franchise offer you have. Here are a few popular ad outlets for franchise ads:

*Wall Street Journal*
*New York Times*
*Los Angeles Times*
*San Francisco Chronicle*
*Chicago Tribune*
*Dallas News*
*Miami Herald*
*Modern Franchising* magazine
*International Wealth Success*
*Specialty Salesman and Franchise Opportunities* magazine

As a guide to where you should advertise, ask yourself:

(1) Who is the "perfect" franchisee?
(2) What newspapers and magazines does he read?
(3) How can my ads best appeal to him?
(4) When is he most receptive to ads?

Knowing the answers to these questions will help you pick your advertising outlets for your franchise.

Should you use an advertising agency? The answer to this question depends on your previous experience in the business world.

If you don't know anything about ads, employ an ad agency. The fee for their service will come out of the cost of your ad, except for any costs of type, artwork, photos, or engravings, which are extra.

But if you know something about advertising, I recommend that, at the start, you write your own ads. You'll quickly learn which features of your franchise offer have the strongest appeal to prospects. This knowledge will be a valuable asset if you ever have to do any face-to-face selling of your franchise offer.

You can, if you wish, have the publication set the type for your ad. This is termed a "pub-set" ad. There usually is *no* charge for this service. However, you may be required to pay for the ad *before* it appears in print.

Radio and TV ads are not too widely used for franchise sales. The reason for this is that the time required to convey the message to the prospective franchisee is too long for the usual ad rates charged on radio and TV. Publication advertising—newspapers, magazines, etc.—is usually more economical for most franchisors.

## HAVE YOUR FRANCHISEES HELP YOU

*Nothing succeeds like success.* Once you have a successful franchisee, get him to tell his friends about his success. Pay him a finder's fee for every prospect he sends to you who buys a franchise. Your finder's fee can range from 2 percent to 10 percent of the franchise price, depending on how anxious you are to sell a franchise.

When you have your franchisees recommend prospects to you, your franchise business can expand by internal growth. There's no better way to grow because internal growth is:

- Low cost
- Easier to control
- Almost certain to provide better franchisees
- Probably one of the best ways to grow

## TAILOR YOUR FRANCHISE TO LOCAL CONDITIONS

Conditions vary from one state to another and from one country to another. If you are to go national and international with your franchise, as I hope you will, you must recognize and allow for different local conditions.

Try to tailor your franchise, where possible and necessary, to local:

- Language differences
- Diet preferences
- Business laws and practices

Conforming to local customs will put money into your pocket and in your franchisee's pocket. So vary your franchise details to conform to local habits but retain the essential characteristics of your franchise at all times. Thus, a Howard Johnson's still retains its orange roof color, colonial architecture, and many-flavored ice creams even though the language spoken in its restaurant and printed on its menu may not be English, but Spanish, French, or Swedish.

## DEVELOP RELATED PRODUCTS

Once you have one franchisee you can start exploring other products or services he might offer or sell besides the basic one offered by your franchise. Use this approach regardless of your ultimate customers—be they the:

- General public
- Owners of special businesses
- Special people you've sought out

Thus, you can sell, at little extra cost, many related items in your franchise, such as:

- Candy in a food franchise
- Model cars in an auto muffler franchise
- Polishing wax in a car wash franchise
- Jewelry in a clothing franchise

Selling other products in your franchise can zoom your profits. In some franchise operations the income from fringe items equals that from the basic franchise!

## DIVERSIFY YOUR BUSINESS

You *can* get rich just selling franchises. But to protect yourself against a fall off in your franchise sales, you ought to have two or more offers going at the same time. Thus, you might first sell a franchise and then sell products to your franchisee. Or you might have your franchisees sell other items for you, which you find for them. You could collect a commission on the sales of these items.

What I'm advising here is a technique that has made me a million dollars from various business activities:

> Keep two or more sources of income active at the same
> time and there's an excellent chance that you'll hit the
> big money quickly and easily.

So diversify—preferably into many different business activities. That way you'll never have to worry about money again!

### Get more people to build your wealth

As many people who read my various money books published by Parker Publishing Company, Inc., and International Wealth Success, Inc., know, I travel throughout the world on business deals. On these trips, I meet hundreds of businessmen and business women in plush offices, exclusive hotels, restricted-membership country clubs, posh restaurants, intimate hideaways aboard gold-plater yachts, on secluded islands in the Baltic, and in the beautiful mountains of continental Europe.

Whenever and wherever I meet these wealthy, never-need-worry people—be it Palm Beach, London, Rome, Los Angeles, Paris, Copenhagen, San Francisco, Stockholm, Brussels, or San Juan—I think of *you, my reader.* I think: "What can I learn from this person, or persons, or situation, that I can pass on to my money-book readers to help them earn more?" (I don't have to try to learn for myself because I've made it big doing my own thing.)

One major fortune-building method which I've seen used profitably in every country, city, and town I've ever visited is:

> To build great wealth, use other people to expand your skills and increase your income and profits.

When you have other people working to build *your* profits, you:

- Earn more per business hour
- Develop more profitable ideas
- Widen your knowledge and skills

The idea of using more people to build *your* wealth is a successful concept in all *usual* businesses. However, this idea does not always work well where your income is earned from a unique talent such as writing, painting, sculpture, and other arts where just *your* abilities are involved. Using more people when you are an artist or creative thinker of some sort is generally best *only* in the sales and promotion areas. With such a scheme:

- You concentrate on production of the product—be it a book, painting, or other creative work
- Certain helpers promote you and your work in the press and elsewhere.
- Other, or even the same, helpers sell your output to dealers, the public, and other buyers.

With this plan you are freed of the grubby details of marketing your products. Further, you can concentrate on what you do well while others spend their time on what *they* do well. You produce more, sell more, and earn higher profits with fewer headaches.

In any franchised business you can do the same, using more people. Thus, you can use people to:

- Sell franchises for you
- Search for, and find, new products
- Develop good ideas you have
- Operate franchises for you
- Write ads and promotion material
- Consult with prospects

Of course, there are many other tasks which you can have suitable people perform for you. To be certain that you don't forget these tasks, prepare a list of them now while you're thinking about them.

### Get synergy to multiply your fortune

With synergy, $1 + 1$ can equal 4, instead of 2. "How can this be?" you ask. Here's how, as given in the definition for synergy:

> Synergy in business is the bringing together of people or firms, or both, having different ideas, backgrounds, skills, and methods for the purpose of solving a specific problem—such as building a more profitable business, finding new customers, and similar expansion operations.

Synergy really works! You *can* get such amazing results that the output of two people, $1 + 1$, equals the output of four people. So, $1 + 1 = 4$, when you are getting synergistic results from your people who are working on your franchise problems.

Now let me give you an important tip based on my experience with synergy. It is:

> Use the skills and know-how of all kinds of people in your franchise work. Try, whenever possible, to hire and use the skills of the poor, the underprivileged, the down-trodden, and the handicapped. These people will give you the synergy and profits you seek!

In my many franchise business activities around the world, this technique has worked beautifully (and very profitably) for me. Since it has been so rewarding for me, I'm certain that it will also be for you, because you're every bit as smart as—or smarter than—I am. I've found that people who haven't had too much in life:

- Work harder for *you*
- Think longer, more deeply, *for you*
- Have greater *practical* creativity
- Can bring a *wider* background into play *for you*

So look widely for your helpers. You'll find that they'll build your franchise profits quickly and surely because synergy will be working for you. I'm a believer in worldwide riches opportunities which *you* build from franchise operations with little or no investment of your own. So let's get started, here and now! You now know:

- What you need to start a franchise business *(an idea)*
- Advantages of franchising *(many)*
- What you can franchise *(plenty of businesses)*
- Useful reference books to help you
- How to learn from other successful franchisors
- What makes a successful franchise idea
- Nine magic steps for getting started in franchising—idea, price, publicity, training, services, uniqueness, advertising, study courses, and testing
- Selling your franchise successfully
- Successful sales techniques for franchisors
- Profitable ways to help franchisees
- How to expand your business *and* your income
- Having franchisees help you
- Diversifying for more profits
- Multiplying your fortune with synergy

### How beginners build success in franchising

I know hundreds of folks who've made it big in franchising their business ideas. Most of these people:

- Started small
- Stayed in one state at the start
- Used borrowed money to begin
- Grew fast once they got going

Here are some franchises that have grown from a small start to a healthy business.

### SAILBOATS FOR HIRE AND FOR SALE

Sailing is one of the most popular sports in the world today. Yet most people:

- Can't afford a sailboat
- Dislike the maintenance
- Just want to sail in the summer
- Need lessons in sailing

Dan Z., a sailing enthusiast, analyzed this situation and decided that a combined sailing-school sailboat-charter franchise might work. A careful study of the market soon revealed that it was much bigger than anyone realized. Dan started his franchise business and within a few months it was a booming success.

In the same field—recreational boating—a yacht-broker franchise begun by a beginner is doing extremely well. All the franchisee needs is a desk and a telephone because the franchisor furnishes a list of boats for sale. A commission is paid by the seller of the boat on each sale. The largest part of his commission goes to the franchisee who makes the sale but the franchisor also receives a small part of the commission, giving him a continuing income.

## FAST FOODS PAY OFF

People never give up eating until the day they take their final, one-way ride out of this world. And eating habits have changed. More people:

- Eat simpler foods
- Enjoy eating out
- Look for lower-cost meals

These changes have led to the boom in fast-food franchises such as McDonalds, Kentucky Fried Chicken, Sizzler, Howard Johnson's, Carvel, Chicken Delight, and the rest.

To make money in franchised fast foods, you must have something different. Thus, another fried chicken franchise would probably have tough going today. But an unusual and tasty food such as Indian curry, might find a booming market. So if you're interested in fast foods, keep an eye open for new foods that might catch the public fancy.

Carl K. took this advice and developed a string of taverns serving hot sliced meat sandwiches. These sandwiches and the few simple side dishes—potato salad, cole slaw, and beans—make the simplest menu known. Yet by locating his franchises in the business districts, Carl was able to attract large lunch-time crowds of businessmen wanting a fast lunch and willing to pay a top price for it.

Today Carl is planning to expand his fast food franchise. But instead of opening more taverns, Carl plans to sell frozen sandwiches by mail order. He thinks that many of his business customers would love to have one or more of his sandwiches on the weekend. Sold 12 or more at a time packed in dry ice, all the buyer need do is pop the sandwich into the oven for a few minutes. Carl is hoping that the wives and kids start eating his sandwiches, too! This would be particularly pleasing to Carl because he started his franchise business on $5,000 of borrowed money.

## AUTO REPAIRS PAY OFF

At any one time there are about half as many autos in the United States as there are people. So autos—and particularly their repair—are *big* business.

Stan L. found this was so when he started a franchise for local car tuneup in your own garage or driveway. The idea for this franchise came to Stan while he was driving to check out a completely unrelated business. Seeing all the cars on the road, it occurred to Stan that their tuneup must be a big business. But every owner had the problem of:

- Finding a good mechanic
- Getting the car to the shop or station for the tuneup
- Not having the use of the car during the tuneup
- Getting home or to work after dropping off the car for tuneup

Acting on these ideas, Stan decided to start a franchise offering:

- Reliable mechanics
- Tuneups in your own garage or driveway
- Work done at *your* convenience
- Guaranteed results

Each tuneup could include an oil change, grease job, points, plugs, condenser, state inspection, and related adjustments. The mechanic would use a specially equipped panel truck as his "roving garage."

To get his franchise going, Stan contacted a local car dealer for estimates on a panel truck. He was surprised at the very low price he'd have to pay for the truck. The same was true of the tuneup equipment needed for the truck. And joy of joys, everything—truck, equipment, ads for the franchise, printing, and the rest—could be done on credit.

Stan priced his franchise at $10,000 and sold 11 in three days after placing his first ad. Today Stan has a whole string of successful auto tuneup franchises in his area. Yet he started with:

- No money
- No "connections"
- No friends
- Just a good idea!

And *you* can do the same—or more—if *you* start with a good idea and plenty of drive. Try for yourself and see!

## POINTS TO REMEMBER

- Franchising your ideas, methods, or other business techniques can build millions from pennies.
- Where there's a market for a product or service, there's a franchise possibility.
- In franchising you can learn a lot by watching what the other guy is doing.
- Help your franchisees as much as you can and they'll help you!
- Develop related franchise products whenever you can.
- Use synergy to build and expand your wealth.

## HELPFUL MONEY BOOKS

Here are a number of useful money books which can help *you* build your riches faster and easier. You will, I believe, profit enormously from reading these books because each one will give you profitable business ideas or methods which can pay off for you in a short time. For, as Aldous Huxley said: "Every man who knows how to read has it in his power to magnify himself, to multiply the ways in which he exists, to make his life full, significant, and interesting." Don't *you* want to make *your* life better, starting now? If so, read these books.

### Available from Prentice-Hall Inc., Englewood Cliffs, N.J. 07632

Bockl—*How Real Estate Fortunes Are Made*, $8.95.

Bockl—*How to Use Leverage to Make Money in Local Real Estate*, $7.95.

Bohon—*Complete Guide to Profitable Real Estate Leasing*, $8.95.

Childs—*Long-Term Financing*, $19.95.

Cossman—*How I Made $1,000,000 in Mail Order*, $8.95.

Friedman—*Handbook of Real Estate Forms*, $16.00.

Hagendorf—*Tax Guide for Buying and Selling a Business*, $19.95.

Kent—*How to Get Rich in Real Estate*, $7.95.

McMichael & O'Keefe—*How to Finance Real Estate*, $10.00.

Paige—*Complete Guide to Making Money with Your Ideas and Inventions*, $7.95.

P-H Editorial Staff—*Encyclopedic Dictionary of Real Estate Practice*, $29.95.

Semenow—*Questions and Answers on Real Estate*, 7th Ed., $9.95.

Winter—*A Complete Guide to Making a Public Stock Offering*, $19.95.

### Available from International Wealth Success, Inc., P.O. Box 186, Merrick, N.Y. 11566

*Financial Broker-Finder-Business Broker-Consultant Course*, $99.50.

*Franchise Riches Course*, $99.50.

*Real Estate Fortune Builders Course*, $99.50.

*"Starting Millionaire" Program*, $99.50.

*Zero-Cash Success Techniques Course*, $99.50. (Includes 1-hour Ty Hicks tape cassette on "Small Business Financing.")

*Mail Order Riches Program*, $99.50.

*Worldwide Riches Opportunities*, Vol. 1. 2500 Leads to Getting Rich in Export-Import Without Leaving Your Own Home, $25.

*Worldwide Riches Opportunities*, Vol. 2. Includes Overseas Lenders Who Will Finance Your Exports. $25.

*How to Prepare and Process Export-Import Documents:* A Completely Illustrated Guide, $25.

*How to Borrow Your Way to Real Estate Riches,* $15. (Compiled by Ty Hicks)

*Small Business Financing:* A 1-Hour Tape Cassette Featuring Ty Hicks in Person, $10.

*Zero-Cash Takeovers of Business and Real Estate,* $25.

*Business Capital Sources,* $15. Lists more than 2,000 business lenders.

*Small Business Investment Company Handbook,* $15. Lists SBIC's.

*Directory of 2,500 Active Real Estate Lenders,* $25.

*Handbook of Successful Borrowing Techniques for Business,* $25.

*Inter-Business Financing,* $15.

*How to Get Venture Funds for Business,* $25.

*Make a Fortune as a Licensing Agent,* $15.


## Available from Parker Publishing Co., Inc., West Nyack, N.Y. 10994

Burleigh—*Double Your Money in Six Years,* $7.95.

Dowd—*How to Earn a Fortune and Become Independent in Your Own Business,* $7.95.

Hicks—*How to Borrow Your Way to a Great Fortune,* $7.95.

Hicks—*How to Build a Second-Income Fortune in Your Spare Time,* $7.95.

Hicks—*How to Start Your Own Business on a Shoe String and Make Up to $100,000 a Year,* $7.95.

Hicks—*Magic Mind Secrets for Building Great Riches Fast,* $7.95.

Hicks—*Smart Money Shortcuts to Becoming Rich,* $7.95.

Kahm—*101 Businesses You Can Start and Run with Less Than $1,000,* $6.95.

Oleksy—*1,000 Tested Money-Making Markets for Writers,* $7.95.

Sarnoff—*Getting Rich with OPM,* $7.95.

Steinberg—*Mortgage Your Way to Wealth,* $8.95.

Steward—*Money-Making Secrets of the Millionaires,* $7.95.

Stockwell & Holtje—*101 Ways to Make Money in Your Spare Time, Starting with Less Than $100,* $7.95.

van Vogt—*The Money Personality,* $7.95.

# Index